C000227148

STEVE GRIFFITHS was born in An; a beach, lived in London most of his Ludlow. He has published seven coll with Rex Collings, Seren and Cinnar *Poems* (Cinnamon Press, 2016). You can see filmed performances of the *Late Love Poems*, for which he received Arts Council England funding, on YouTube. His work has been widely broadcast and he has read in several countries, including a series of seven readings in New York in 2012. He is one of the hundred twentieth century Welsh poets writing in English featured in The Library of Wales 'Poetry 1900-2000' (2007, Parthian Books). He has a collection of new poems up his sleeve. He worked first as a welfare rights and community worker, then as a researcher and policymaker in social and health inequality. Working for central Government at the turn of the century, he was an architect of a billion-pound investment in supported housing while working at weekends on his poetic exploration of a fallible Utopia, *An Elusive State*. He later wrote studies on reducing emergency hospital admissions. He still publishes the occasional policy thinkpiece online. And he's a proud grandad. His poetry website is www.stevegriffithspoet.com.

Critical Responses to Steve Griffiths' Collections

"It's a parallel universe, a magical epic, a comfort, a mystery."
BBC Producer Laura Thomas, on *An Elusive State*, 2007

"An Elusive State is a poetic epic of time, place and language…both as invented as More's original Utopia, and as real as the small town on Anglesey where Griffiths was born…a distinctive, distinguished accomplishment…truly a parable of many parallels, one for and beyond our times…"
Amanda Hopkinson, *Planet*, 2009

"Challenging, refreshing…the tangential world we really inhabit… ambitious, demanding… The book has a strong and well maintained intellectual thrust which frankly sets it apart from much modern poetry. Al-Chwm itself flickers before us like a mirage, but changes shape as the next poem arrives. In the end…we must realise that the people these ambitious and challenging poems describe are ourselves, and that they represent the permanently unsettled (and unsettling) human imagination. The book is a quest, and for every reader that quest will have a different result. Maybe that is its great value."
Robert Minhinnick, on *An Elusive State*, 2008

"Late Love Poems explores what is timeless about love but also those qualities of sexuality, pain, devotion and grief that are affected by the ageing process… It presents an intimate diary of love which explores the rhythms of living with someone, cooking with someone, sleeping with someone… Ultimately, though Griffiths' collection challenges one age-old stereotype – that love is the domain of the young – it is unable to deny the other: love cannot make us immortal."
Katya Johnson, Poetry Wales, 2017

WEATHEREYE: SELECTED POEMS

Patchworks

of Amlwch,
a pattern of fields and buildings
interlocking with lives
                    that drift
and jolt down centuries

in conflict and agreement,
through the blind accelerations of history,
the growth of poems,
the advance and retreat of peoples,

personal defeat and victory.
Like others before me
I make shift among scatterings
of lived material:

first when the system of *cymorth*, mutual help
precluded the need for a Poor Rate
in the unbroken tradition of the farming hamlet
its innocence broken by copper;

then through the mining boom
when a sympathetic priest
petitioned for the injured
to the agent of Lord Anglesey

and through the simultaneous trough of the wave:
a hut full of naked children
destitute of all conveniences
and almost all necessities

a patchwork of rags to be coveted
under the threat of the red cloth badge
of dependence on the parish –
beginnings of the red menace in Wales.

In the wake of those years,
the visiting of the people
with a winter of cholera.

In the good times, neighbourly
hogs rooted at liberty in the streets.

Now we have tourism,
materially paper-thin,
letting in the light.

Patchworks of Amlwch,
a pattern of fields and buildings
interlocking with lives.

You stood at the edge of the colour, slight,
but there, as by the ballroom floor you might
have wanted to impress some well-lined beau.
Our minds moved together, a moment shared.
You would have shuddered at the intimacy.
You had bought this view. A carriage waited
on the mountainside, to remove it from you.

I carried our intimacy back to the van,
a fragment of eggshell,
a peasant savouring the illicit
with a little smile of gratification.
Your driver too was waiting,
with his patient, leathery face,
an impenetrable landscape.

Cemaes Songs

1

A girl of fourteen
forbidden the barbecue
by her father the minister –

I remember her laugh and her touch;
a sharp unfulfilled memory.
I was seventeen.

I think she played the violin.

2

The ruddy cheeks, the bright eyes,
not wine but whisky,

an unconscious classical pose:
a boy, a drunk scrum-half
on a rock, looks at the horizon.

A transistor competes with the hush of the sea.

The hands plashing, the squeals
of the naked swimmers:
bathsounds, half-echoed, innocents.

3

The morning's incredible clarity:
the sea could be ruefully subdued,
but its one eye glitters still.

The refuse man with his bag picks his way
along the tide-edge, bending at intervals.
The aftermath of a party, nothing stale.

Mona's owners

Iron age hollows of soft grass.
Bracken, blazons of gorse.

Innocent hollows, tolerated
by the legionary: superannuated communes,

how could they live
without walls and mosaic aspirations?

A ragged ineffectual priesthood, too close
to the turf: its circular homes and songs

have always existed, touched to conscious use
by a minuscule timespring of history:

distanced by wind, strangely ennobled
by filth, outflanked by a literate efficiency.

Christmas Night

Like the clear sound of crushed snow underfoot,
my pen hangs on the immediate past.

A muffler of wind wraps round the sturdy caravan.
Shadows of raspberry canes in my mother's garden

fall across my thoughts.   Stars are laid out
in their impeccably timed wait

for my discovery of the random.
Snows of clarification, newsreels of memory

cover my lines.   By morning
there are new impassable hills, new transparencies.

I did not understand how so holy a man
as the Bishop could discuss the weather
with the organist.

Morning.
Every boat sunk.
An amazed, exhausted silence.
The wind still rushing determined
to compensate for its vacuums.

Backward glances

Returning, I live with a huge space
at my shoulder
and a light step.
A bird is a white arc
whose call forges a slit in the dome.
Memories and future pour in.

A rabbit, its eyes and ears swollen and senseless,
lollops across our path.
These elements have coincided:
now the sea has lapped these fired grains
we can act or die.

The sea fits the coast precisely from moment to century.

My mind fits the strong exhalations of the surf.

Patterns of history, smallest events
in the folding of mountains.
Someone loses a satchel.
He reappears in a teashop
with a wife smilingly pregnant.
Names from my class
appear on competition charts
on the wall of a bar-room.
I pass through, my significance is
a commercial transaction for bitter.
My eyes alive in the fingers of time,
powerless as the sheep beaten into pens at the market.

In the port, a man eats chips casually

in the wheelhouse of the oil terminal tug,
among the deaths of landscapes and crafts.

Tired empty accidents give form to the future.

People with shit on their hands labour
with their capacity to change

their sharpest perceptions half-lit
and half-blinded with shit.

To make progress is not to play in the light
but it is to choose the light

to leave no energy unturned
in the darkness of history.

Our minds are cleared with the water of sources.

May the trees bend and spring back.

Trees in your garden shade your salad and wine

Trees in your garden shade your salad and wine.

Our eyes and our fingers run over each other.
Our bodies fly into the trees.

The branches bend nervously, in the afternoon.

They haven't seen anything like your absolute smile,
your toes in my hair.

They marvel at the rough inflection of your nipples,
and again

your smile that opens windows where there are no houses.

Everyone watches the sunset

Everyone watches the sunset
in airport lounges waiting, groups that compose
themselves and rotate, clutching souvenirs and small change.

I carry your rough sparrowquick laugh
from the small hours,
bars of copper light from your fine hair.

In the train that carries you away
among clusters of words thrown casually
together like exiles

I could be the sound of birds beyond the window,
the shadow on the carriage wall,
wearing your hat.

Burning the stubble

1

The spears and the wings of the maize
in stillness and in wind

find their celebration

and the black and the fiery cumulus towering,
the thunder asleep in its arms.

I pad to a hilltop
poplars bandaged in mist.

The woman in my bed dreams
aloud of calm, shifting

through vacated territory.

2

The voices in the grass are whirring
at the cries in the heat

the smoke at the throat catching:

a cicada hollowed out by systematic ants
my cigarette burning on the road

there will be more burning,
more pests and husks
but the maize reminded me
how the ground's for turning.

At the Consecration

The wind tugged at our starched surplices
in the stream of evening sun.
The Bishop of Bangor strode at our head
with his golden mitre to the House of God,
solidly, and belted the door.
Given admittance, we took to the aisle,
trying not to wobble as we walked
but to move as on Lewis's escalator
in Liverpool, with single-minded symmetry.
The wind rose. We sang, impressed
with the ritual electricity. The wind rose.
Big Chris got episcopal dispensation
to relieve his bleeding nose.
The darkness thickened, the wind
strained at the windows, a door at the back
broke open. Four men heaved to shut it.
Our wide eyes swallowed our concentration,
our faces burning, our music sheets stirring.

Creak of cargo shift.
Smallness of the collective voice
struggling through the service,
for those in peril on the sea.

Suddenly in the roof a skylight crashed,
the church was filled with a mighty rushing wind
from a square of blackness
that sucked us towards it.
This was the Consecration.

After God had visited,

now he takes lengthy siestas
and talks of reconstruction.
Mummy is beautiful.
She presides anxiously.

In your next picture,
your first communion,
you make a run for it
bored and sweaty
in your biting petticoat

setting the stamp on your future.
Under her veil, your mother's glance
of fire: the firm hand laced
with exquisite piety;
the nip of her fingernail.

With its loving dedication scored through,
on the following page I found
an insupportable portrait
with a little narrow triumphant smile
that knows there's never long to wait:

a couple cut into relief,
one holding the scissors blindly,
one enduring without a sound.
The moments are thrown on the table,
the possessed faces called into formation.

You join me in some terminal, as always
like a closing of unnatural spaces.
Teenagers queue at the picture kiosk
with lovely assumptions of poise.
You're clutching the empty faces

of a prisoner with the bitter innocence

of a foreign girl in a foreign town
where hands reach out from the shadows
and nothing moves but a tape
left running over tense-lipped silence.

There are so many words for you
and I am constantly grasping them,
as many nervous eyes on history,
so many botanical terms never
known in a massive English landscape.

You pass by, breathing life into mirrors.
This time I touch you, a small
unknown moment, a small unidentified
flower verging on the miraculous
but particular, and asleep under great trees.

The galleons drive through the channel
with so many powers and fragilities.

A few bars over again

The surfaces of childhood
pulse with what lured us
to what we became:

this blinding light full of motion
brimming with plankton and fire
this concentration the purer
for being only physical, over a shallow pool
with a fine net, shadowing transparent prawns

this village festival too perfect
for the surrounding years,
a mirage in time towed on a string
through the shoals of disillusion
and the demands of family closing in

this adult too self-important
to stop slapping his big wet threshing fish
of words across the retreated room,
watched by a child who will always now
be poised in a half-open frustrated silence.

We catch ourselves playing over
these moments, a few bars at a time
without touching the keys.
We learn how to paint the sky
in a thousand ways

without ripping through to the original.
Your villages of painted clay lead sinuously home,
this series of windows penetrated

by an experimental light, this green against
blue that records a path overgrown or a strong dream,

this innocent wall against which
people are never lined up and shot
or if they are, the sky-blue wall
is marked like chance leaves with the quiet
spatter of a primal atrocity.

Then the need for a real house and a real
child crosses the old light.
Smears of an earthly innocence deepen
in your shadow, proscribing the past
like the light brush of a vapour trail

on a pre-industrial morning.
You move upstream, motors open,
languages falling off you like sweat.
Houses call out from within you
to be given form and firmly ripen.

Courage

The baby's harelip's darned brilliantly
like the hospital sheets he lies on.
Wards close
and the nurses grow fierce, unnoticed.

Arms outspread in splints
as if for flight, his gums are bared
as his mother, his dependable
aviary of mobiles, and his father
move the other side of his tears.

His blood is bright as an old man's,
the incision part of my acute past,
the nerves run bent over double
when I think of it.
I'm not helping, how could I,
wearing the badge of his lip
as he walks through my dream,
eyes and hands alight, chuckling
at his mother who leans over him
in a little storm of generosity.

The baby grins briefly
at his own strength
through his pain,
the first mirror.

Community, 1982

                              among the multitudes
Of that great City, oftentimes was seen
Affectingly set forth, more than elsewhere
Is possible, the unity of man,
One spirit over ignorance and vice
Predominant, in good and evil hearts;
One sense for moral judgments, as one eye
For the sun's light.

Wordsworth, The Prelude, Book Eighth, ll823-830

My nose angles the air,
a little missile edged into the sunset,
little receiver, the indigenous one
who doesn't belong,
sensing an odour of fascism
round a lack of generosity
like the swelling round an inoculation
gone wrong.

Newspapermen prowl the dusk
attacking strangers,
ribbing out their flesh
which hangs in colours on the line
to warn of habitation and strict ways.
In the ensuing dark, queues form
for doctors.

But this old basement laundry fought for,
the washing-slabs gone
with grandmother's solid arms;
then control of it,

a community centre
bandaged with posters,
playgroups fought for –
and why not, for every child,
a possibility and an open door?

Shrinking horizon

In a public darkness
private stars glimmer behind a curtain.
Darkness pours at the windows
off buildings close by.

If I retired to watch
the brighter moments at a distance
I would seek myself out in exile,
accused of dereliction.

They are closing the children's wards,
they are breaking up the future.
A pile of agendas
in a buzzing, dirty twilight.

We slide back the decades
to the big stones on the roof of the moor.
I sit watching them
with my small clerical hands,

Stonehenges that never transcended
the weather's disorder.
The lean wolf's breath on the white neck
guarantees a tomorrow.

A Spanish Providence

Under the muscled limbs
of the flowering chestnut
you coil,
snoozing near to the roots
and the follicles where I begin.

I look up through the serpentine
branches: fingertunnels,
green bottlenecks furnish
scented rooms whose
flowered paper shifts soothingly.

You seem to have spun down
through these folded vistas
from the little spoiling solicitudes
for butter and cream, security,
best lace and frivolity

that cushion you, peeping
and smiling as a child
in a post-war Austerity photograph.
The opposition have been eliminated.
A vigorous blade

on a bare hill,
Daddy smiles the victor's
casual, masculine smile,
thrusting out of the stubborn
privation of war.

Daddy is vindicated:

Like beasts

Rats out of market,
the warheads are camped in the fields of Suffolk.

The crops are lit up.
My face is turned toward heaven.

The trumpets of valium excite us to war.
Columns of casings will bubble and peel.

They will devour Kiev
and be spectacular over England.

The expected wind in the chimney.
My gaze turns inward, hesitant.

One year old, my son smiles at every gust.
The seasons turn quickly now,

they scar my hands like a wheel.

Post imperial

Reggae thumps, a hangover,
fruit and meat drumming the ground
in a rumour from the imperial past.

An elm stands like a fishbone in midsummer.
The cats fornicate in its barbed shadow,
the lean strays motored for lust.

The sweatshops are gutted,
their staircases hung like tongues.

A bank signals from the City's towers,
a computation to the bare threshing-floor,
the Christmas light to the vacated room.

The moon hangs in the elm
like a hat hung on justice.

A man waits for a bus that never comes
there are drunks drunk with waiting
for history as it goes past their noses,
rolling unevenly like a ball on the cobbles,
there are drunks starved of the evidence
in streets full of ghosts.

The perversion of development,
the memory of industry
tranquillise the place
out of its present,

so noisy, so gone,

florid with dogshit, dotted
with cartons on vacant lots
and the refuse of casual acts.

Hairdresser, age 55, Dalston

Her fingers dart over terraced streets
mortared with lacquer.

Her house was a ship into another world.
Skinheads rucked past her draped lace curtains
leaving a smudge on the air,
high on aeroplane glue,
running feet, swung pipework, thuds
that vibrated the window-frames like a truck.

The humming ranks of driers,
the tang of shampoo,
her royal texts,
the husbands at the threshold, there to collect.

Her incorruptible trinkets,
her white arms working.
Her dustsheet silence,
her practised chatter along rails.
Her canyons.
Her kindness to dogs.
Her close things.

I heard a delicious solitude,
soaping itself, in her lonely bathsounds.
The white, wrinkled pore-stars of her imagination
a white bear undiscovered, echoing
contentedly in a white pool.

And I see her taking vengeance
on what others have made:

the bent necks of the skinheads
under the rod of her avenging alabaster angel,
the Victorian terraced hillway to the pit,
their faces turned upwards,
their arms laid aside,
urged onward by uniformed guards.

Watching riot

I saw the tall graceful one who ran
like a dancer carrying a vase
with his plastic bag and its glue and fumes
held precious and still,

the other arm swinging an empty bottle
which he bowled at a caricature
of a shopkeeper in a white coat
who shook his British-passported fist

and whose legs trembled on for hours.
So he took stock of the dried goods,
the repetition holding him together.

My son stood by his tricycle,
admired the energy of the swung brightness
and the delicious ice-splatter of glass

and practised the overarm action afterwards.

Union leader, services rendered

So you finally found peace
in this rural obsolescence
outside the familiar country
where so little was held with a fierce defence.

And though you supported them steadfastly,
you thought, you never meant there to be
no choice but for good and all,
no plane waiting at the airport.

Your feet stuck in the honeyed morass of history
now you move at a geological pace.
You turn and eye the House of Lords,
askance, with some respect, then sweating quietly

as the dew, you arrive at the antic showcase:
dripping bats in a cave. A balloon of words
in the comics you learned to read from,
commitments dissolve on your lips, and already

the Miners' Gala beats a forgotten drum.
Though in an uncarpeted corner of your eye bobs
the faceworkers' light that gave you momentum,
coaldust fades beyond the recall of your feet.

Through interference from other gobs
stuffed with the earth of their English shires,
broadcast, your tongue is a leaf compressed
with a mouthful of peat.

Education

Old, mad, dancing Mrs. Dean
celebrated the expiring candle
of her eighty years
with three kids from the estate,
whose harassing fingers
scrabbled like rats and draughts
in the space between doorframe and wall.

'Who shall I vote for?'
she asked me
when I told her she could,
'they're all smilin' 'addocks'.

Bitten with inspiration
she put a match to the crack.
A scream.
Next day they were back.

Glyndŵr Subdued

Burned out, there was no road back,
and the flames of Sycharth brought Glyndŵr
dreams enough:
his home was a country now,
the revenges multiplied.
The helicopter's shadow,
a great hare
runs fleetingly across a field –
the grass panicking, flattened,
trying to disperse but unable.

Almost an experiment,
the disciplined ructions of the first raid,
the strained respect for brawny lives
a delicate line: Rhuthun settlers,

robbed and dishevelled, emerged
to a heady, bright, small Welsh triumph
reeking of sheepshit
and soot in the bright sun:

insults counted, it was a homely,
small, scared, village altercation
as shoving and grunting skirmishes
around slag once made history.

The victors clattered away
shod heavily with expensive curses
to where even the sparks on the hill
were drunk down by the mud and the dark.

Later the conscripts, cast-off and dangerous,
sported their rusted dream of omnipotence,
hacking for their neglected fields
and their friends cut down,

and then for the riven cold in their bones
women ran in the wet grass
brought down like deer with cries of triumph.
People ran blindly,

made his, the pervasive guerilla
reeking of smoke and prophecy,
the peaceloving fire
displaced in his rafters.

The banging of shields,
plastic and leather,
rang in his ears:

war war war sle sle sle
went the childish wailing of sirens
in the gusting wood,

and the night's drunken instruments
scoured the wet streets
for the Welsh doggis and their whelps.

An English city listens behind curtains
to the running and breathing, the slugging
thud of quarry cornered and floored:

the resistance is
that we will not turn the television up
in tribute to the night.

Divided loyalties, undermined
meal-tickets, sprouted on hillsides,
the weeds Indignation
twined with deep-rooted Ambivalence

picked for the same dish.
Drenched resisters sidled in droves
along valleys to give themselves up
to the straggling columns of troops and grain.

When the fighting is over, the land of dreams
is a table lit with unshareable faces,
a once-in-a-lifetime
remembered meal to the hungry:

a looted peacock under the arm
of some big, sharp-featured
father of mine
who dried his eyes at the flame of Sycharth.

Then the withdrawal to memory
of the fair people, walled in the clouds
of exile within, the retreat to mystery
of the fair times on their vague upland tracks.

Glyndŵr had to master this potent
trick of retirement, to the light
in a dolmen glimpsed rarely and late,
a light in the mind

where sometimes he lingers noisily in the grid of years
and the speed and charisma growl in him
to the applause of the shingle in the undertow,
old chimera whose wait has a tide's hypnotic

push still. It breaks
in like the sudden clatter of leaves
of a kneeling army

or a belief in the mountains upturned,
with mirrors,
lit from inside with our own light.

*The poem uses the chant of the northern English students at Oxford,
heard by Adam of Usk, at the beginning of the Glyndŵr uprising:*

*"War war war, sle sle sle
the Welsh doggis and their whelps".*

Villa-Famès, August 1986

i.m. Fernando Almela, 1943-2009,
and Alberto Solsona, 1943-88, painters

Red, soft-rock strata cut a line
of niches, shelters, age-creases
and navels in dry, strewn terraces
of erosion and collapse.
In hardened powdery space
abandoned to hawks and foxes
we were easily scattered among fossils.
Our voices indiscreetly
defied the undersea silence
among the winds, and were lost.

In a decorated overhang
a chipped half-circle of stick-men
move with serious staves and appetite
through layers of memory and smoke.
It's their blood inundates the streets
from flood-channels high in the town.
With an arrow through him
a bull rears and falls forward
in ochre and blood,
surrounded in the grey bushes.

The afternoon gone badly awry,
firecrackers, beercans and oildrums
crash through the last of the bull's mind.

Neatfooted, barrel-chested, tossing
star on a rope with a minder, he came in
to the faces leaning forward to applaud
and the leafing back of old men

in their irony and knowing pride
for boys their children raised
who stretch and thrust and crow
their hips seasoned with wine and panic.

Their fast trainers touch
the edge of the bull's reach
to provoke the girls with fingers sucked
between their teeth:

the bull keeps coming,
he's a boxer with the odds stacked
and the crowd applaud its dreams,
his breathing
sorely intimate and provoked.

He bursts up the stairs, over a barrier
scattering runners into back yards
breaking sanctuary.
Women wave red towels for him
and he looks for his escape in lizard cracks.

He's down again, quick and light
and goaded by the curious flapping of a hat:
he fills a gap between spars
with his jarring distended trophy of a face.
He leaves a last mark in the wall of a café.

Only his tail and flanks move
and a scribble of flies
that ride his heat.
There's a questioning
unsteady stillness.

Through a field that blossoms handkerchiefs
and hands to catch his eye,

he turns to begin his last passes
to the small men running away
down his long vista.

The halter's ready.
Behind him are stick-men who poke and shout.
A beercan clatters towards him.
A father holds up his little girls to the bull.

He's wound in closer on a line
towards the butcher's laundered shorts.

The murdered bull goes up to the square,
becomes hung meat on a cross,
is elected mayor and presides
over a music shrill, lop-sided, steely
with a movement of hips for his death.
There is subtle food in the clarinet and saxophone,
there are stately dark shades
on dining chairs, dressed for a nativity.
A slow colouring from the throat
of a trumpet hovers round
intimate parts that glisten in buckets
and probably reflect the stars above,
however faintly.

Six fiesta queens relax
beyond the arc lights, lounging
doe-eyed in their self-belief;
six official virgins off-duty,
marriageable somewhere between tonight
and the eighteenth century,
decorated with good hope,
strapping daughters in shawls
of intricate lace,
the village fixed on them

with carnival tenacity
to invest in and honour their vigour
of weathered figureheads
with green shoots and a lick of paint,
their grandmothers' gold combs in their hair.

Through flaking teeth of rock
that lay broken on hillsides
run imprints of movement,
rushes of stone, stills.

A lean fox turns to watch
women once honoured
bury the thin resilience
of their voices in ploughed land.

Dry clouds crackle their long storm
like a leaf in the fist
over a parched line of almonds.

A video trained on coils of blue plumbing
in a bucket by the fountain
summoned the gut-stirring curiosities
of the Civil War:
those farmworkers who carried out
centuries of the bodies of saints and nuns
and arranged them
interestingly, in daylight
in the plenitude of their inheritance.

Scavenging in the early chill of the square
the fox looks up to the silent windows
and the sleepers behind their eyelids of stone
where blood dries quicker than music.

Elegy for John Tripp

A man on the radio talked of soft tissue
printed on million-year riverbed
like a morning-after mattress –
and I thought of you very clear, John,
lifting a pint of dark in some dolmen basement
regarding the sudden answers of the morning
after your stealing away, your sharp face
set in that spirit of mock astonishment
you learned to bewilder
producers of talks and tired assumptions.

I remember a belated urgency
in your face, as it turned back
watching the cultivation of soft edges,
as history, its fares paid, took off like that taxi
you tried to hail with a borrowed carafe.
There was a march full of friends' banners
and irony, probably sodden,
with a brass band and a cock-up somewhere.

On a stand in another world
the unprofitable take an unremitting review
of their leaders.
You take the salute, spilling drinks
and blood and atonement,
and you break the silence
with what nearly everyone felt,
snarling at flummery, throned, waxing manic
then tender as warm buns in a paper bag
with some small forgiven fault
from your recognised gallery.

Confusion and moral astonishment,
something unfinished, an obvious instruction
unlearned: you listened and stirred tea
to the huge roaring ironies
of shopping bag conversation
as the rust-red deep shit rose at the window.

Then you slotted the poems accurately
in the darkness between laughing teeth
in darkened smokefilled rooms
like some young boy who, they said,
had 'immaculate positional play';
like the occasional sun through the steamy
windows of your café,
illuminating the brown sauce and the salt.

And you planted your ground of demands
that you never sold
for one moment of narrow-angled comfort,
brambles round tanks.
Your green armies
knitted their sharp-eyed peace,
needling hard minds,
weaving, digging, planting,
still they work and plot:
they move down out of the hills' cover
laughing their experienced laugh.

Major Powers at Heyford

They vaunt their hammer-drill mastery
across pristine bird-morse, these fighters
on the edge of the continental shelf,
and the mowers' smoothing wash of lawn
and the silent grooms with their horses' sharp steps
pause in respect, watching
trapped birds in the world's house
fly at a mirror.

In Steeple Aston
dumb with its own lush self-esteem
I'm taken back
by a kindly organic thatcher
to the ridge of a garage roof,
clutching my little certainties
like tenuous lichen
as a Vulcan bomber drifts down
slowly enough to think time's stopped,
unicorn-white,
moth-nocturnal with dusted wings,
that fragile.
H-bombs had something special in them
the shape of rugby-posts,
and I knew these Vulcans had them aboard.
I'd heard gunshot from woods
but I knew from the air it was cleaner,
that distance picked things white like the sea,
and cleaner's what we stood for.

Over the fields I ran after the Comet,
the Vampire, the Gloster Javelin

with its camouflage, the lofty things
with hawk-noses, the masked pilot
and helmeted conqueror, Cabbage White,
Tortoiseshell, Red Admiral,
and I collected the cards from packets of tea.

And now it has come to these boys, decked out
in their armour delicate as flies,
bearing their savage captions
from my comic book
that curled brown on the kitchen range –
it's all in there:
the man who blessed the congregation of planes,
the quiet sufficiency of cockpit data,
the editorial decision:
Gadafy's adopted daughter whited out
with the corrosive innocence of distance.

Unmetalled Road

in memory of my father, 1893-1984, composer

He went when I was four:
there were a few stamps from Africa
that bore the reassuring orange tree,
the one I believed money grew on.

Responses are grafted and trained
but they take their own curious flight:
ashes clouding the wind,
they become a shared thing,
a spilled thing.
Like cattle in churned mud,
the wreaths breathe on each other
in a corner of intimate sustenance,
lowing their silent farewell.

The past darkens and advances like a wall,
lightfooted creatures moving behind it.
Old and stooped, he knew the score
and it's buried and his,
music lingering like gas
or a secret body under an old floor.
His city reverberates in taut wood
and burns, it is long gone Belfast,
he takes it with him in a mason's box.

He creeps past my narrow bed
in the dark, looking at me with rare
tenderness among barks of prejudice,
a goblin with the rotating eye of a lighthouse,
a mastery of empty searoads.
The wall holds its breath.

He bobs by on the night
and I try to make of him
something less than a monster,
small but imposing,
appeared suddenly from far out at sea.
Damp-eyed reminiscence floats in, regrets
and boasts each hiding the truth like a room
viewed through glasses of brandy.

Old foghorn on full sail
he goes by grandly preoccupied
with his voices spread along Gothic ceilings
outward like palm leaves in cathedral spaces.

He leaves me with his unvisitable
crag of complaints and psalms
which stand in their own time:

making allowances for age and a thoughtless
and ruthless desire for only the best,
I listen for the quiet haunting of his blood.

The Guesthouse

In a living hold
of legs and table-spars
I hugged my knees and listened
beneath the long table-talk
to the creaking of seasoned joints,
the friction of thighs in nylons,
to my mother's nerve
carrying the spirit of the house
through the stir and grate of coffee-spoons,
the guests diving for wit's minnows,
the spirit of the house carrying her nerve.

The past is swallowed, or crystallised
like laughter caught in the bottom of a cup,
to be washed out or examined
till the particles dance:
the trick pyjama-man hung from a light
who faced the sea in a darkened room,
the laughter that ran down
a sweating kitchen wall
like a thrown egg
or caught the skin like sea-holly
planted between sheets.

After the meal,
we ran with the dogs on the sand,
their pink tongues lolling at speed
past the washed-away gravehill.
Under the sea were the overrun stumps
of a forest, at low water
you could see the swimming heads

of bladderwrack
and this was how the forest of Welsh
drifted away perversely
on an incoming tide,
receding as the rafts crossed Menai,
a waterbird beyond the trees
striking distance and terror
in the invading troops
for this densely populated language
of fogs and yellow grass.
My dogs ran towards it,
barking to enter
through the long sealight,
from the bleached coastways
into the hard bark
and the leaves that drip
their stickiness into open mouths,
but there was nothing where they stood:
oystercatchers quivered their limit
in the tide-edge light.

We blushed with sweat,
spiky-haired and sand-encrusted
in the shop at the end of the beach;
tormented across the sweetjars
by some unattainable thing of
lace and fulsome violets,
her chaste Welsh poise
so very clean, our shyness intact
as tender breasts encased
in the firm imaginary government
that she exercised over us,
we ran back to a vigorous system
of dams and canals
that we built and destroyed repeatedly
from a rivulet that leaked out under a rock

and spread across the sand to meet the tide.
We made a prosperous broad swathe
of yellow crops and minerals
with buried trees and relics,
full of small hidden scenes:

here, a boy looked up at the locomotive
his father, refusing to be lifted up
to the footplate
for the dirty brilliance of the anthracite
that burned with integrity from every face,
and it rode away, taking its power
to be smashed in the waves;
here a boy waved a stick amazed
as the tall cattle sauntered like liners
under his power in deep mud
(here a group at the piano echoed
the suspended bite of good harmony
into gathered corners)

and we yelled as level after level
of our world collapsed
beneath the waves that crashed and curled
over the clouded faces of the lakes –
you could see people running
on the listed decks of a steamer –
we yelled and rebuilt,
the sea at our elbow
sated mischievously
with ships pulled over in the night,
a great sow that smiled and fawned
in the adulterous shallows
that lapped the sand from under her nipples
at dawn, small waves purling over her.

Now, my creations lie about me

in a guest house room,
found and set out
as ornaments of porcelain and brass:
selected acts and losses,
the deceptions
that passed over my head
in a living ship of adults
with the dry pollen of cheek and groin
there among pods dropped
round a vase on a sideboard.
It could be a place of silent attrition
as downstairs the ghosts take tea.

On the cropped, wine-dark lines of the carpet
I push my Maserati to its limit:
how the tyres hold their bends,
the commentary's roared out
to a distant knot of voices
woven with radio choirs
on some bar of time, where rows
of mothers are calling us in
late from the dunes,
where the shell of a church
is sturdily beached,
little humblecake walled round
above the tidal rocks by a testing site,
pointing west out to the migrations.
In the shrunken timber of the door
high-coloured boys in uniform
have gouged and left their mark
beside the grated stones of the bay.
Small yearly services,
the rare flap of a cassock
hold on to a residual power in the air
by what remains of the causeway
there among the disordered shingle.

Turned on the sea,
the land's curved bowl reverberates
after the passage of a fighter.
I add my name and leave
pursuing dishevelled saints
in cauldrons of wind.

The choice of flowers

Through the rain's dissolute footsteps
the town's hum is a thing left on a stove,
beginning to cook on its own.
The call of a Boeing
is a fly that passes in the kitchen.
You are a warm light seen from the street,
but I am inside
and still surprised.
Something strange is happening.
I get off a bus in the wrong place
one midsummer dusk
and follow two strangers down a lane
under cascades of wild grass.
I am having an affair with fiction,
the passings, the shadow-life
of time misplaced.
The man didn't think of the woman
until it was too late.
He only thought of her when he was down,
and the thought uplifted him
and when he saw her again he loved her,
and the years moved him.
And the woman disappeared,
there had been buttonholes and speeches
but no-one there knew
that where she began was much later
when bodies had filled out
and were prone to be comic vehicles
of dignity, courage or regret
and their beauty was a thing
that contained all these.

Someone waves from a life you didn't choose,
from a line of portholes
in a temporary structure,
and you realise the corridor you walk
is a life too.
The trick of familiarity
is a perverse trick,
you are buried in the present,
longing both to rise out of it
and into it.
An illusion of daffodils in the winter gloom
is an act of will or strangeness
and its light underneath your face
makes you look like a ghost.

The Chiming at Trwyn Du

Brilliant as oiled plumage in hollows of sand
at first, the cars' paint
fades in the salt breeze
while their humans peel off into solitude.
The crest of the waves' surge is unbroken,
and the running of the silence is crowned
by the bell off Trwyn Du.
God's cry contracts to a hum
that fades in the current,
there, and there, he cannot
leave it alone, the loud
irregular call of a secretive bird.
There is no passage landward:
we watch, blessed, from the rocks
in the company of the deep-wrinkled mountains.

For the Irish Sea

The sea is increasingly
a desperate metaphor:
the slimy creatures of the spirit
leave the shells of their body
recklessly in the sand;
when other people are beyond us
we retreat to the sea's
invulnerable dells.
Through swirling banks of weed
at their stations, tangle, dulse
and furbelows, through toothed wrack,
knotted wrack, channelled and spiral,
comes the radioactive word
released by the Secretary
for the Environment.
It churns the careless plankton
slowly with a dispassionate tail.
It is an experiment in barbarism,
a progress crowned.
Its fuel is knowledge
we cannot assimilate.
It has an origin to spoil.

The shooting of Levellers, Burford, 1649

From the roof of Burford Church
that served its turn as prison
and grandstand for an exemplary killing,
the final purity of the starlight:
first an idea, yoked with violence together,
then broken up into uncontrollable particles
as in the rasping, visible breath
among three hundred
of Anthony Sedley, sixteen-forty-nine, prisner,
who cut the many short diagonal
scores of his name in the font.
The fires of Cromwell and Fairfax
among the tombs
were will-o'the-wisps grown monstrous,
mocking the name of Sedley
as it drained with the first light,
waiting in all his physical detail,
in the biting of his lip
for the names of the dead.
Sedley, spared:
chosen, Cornet Thompson, Corporal Perkins,
Private Church.
They had no memorial:
Cromwell spoke quietly to them,
this was marked
before they were shot.
In his hurry
he began to cut 'Athony',
and had to go over it.
He had scratched a secret presence,
given time, in the naming of children,

in the renouncing of the vain
pomp and glory of the world
with all covetous desires of the same
and the carnal desires of the flesh,
so that thou wilt not follow
nor be led by them,
to be on the safe side
for Liberty cannot be provided for
in a general sense
if property be preserved.
His balls contracted
for no wonder he hath enemies,
the hairs on his back
raised in each particular.

He walked away unmarked,
his stomach ploughed with fear
across watermeadows,
turning in his mind
the bird that will only fly inside a jar
that awaits a shattering,
a reckoning,
the unbearable rush of freedom:
his name without a gravestone,
in a font.

Commercial

Was this going to sell the beer or the car?

He drove through the rough streets
in an endearing light
of sunset and elderly brick.
His features were delicate
yet incisive, like the car.
His was a rooted
but far-roaming life
with a sliver of unease,
enough sadness to give him depth
but not enough to make him unenviable.
He was driving to the Soldier's Return,
wearing a quality scarf thrown
with timing on a well-cut tweed
to find his father where he left him,
non-verbal, waiting for a pint awkwardly.
He got the pint,
among silenced friends,
a smooth one.
They recognised him as he sat beside his Dad
and looked ahead and they supped.
The car's metallic glint outside,
his capsule with Vivaldi
waiting on the brick road.
The local transmuted to the international,
golden property.

We smiled throughout the cinema.
We felt good about ourselves,
or what we could be, could have been,

or about someone we had known,
not quite ourselves.   And why not?
The Dad's face broke into a smile,
or was about to.

At the post-mortem
the team from Marketing
were breasting the tape again,
riding the crest,
surfing the shit –
and why not?
The creative one
slapped his desk with pleasure.

When the chips are down
whose will they be?

Murder

The wreaths,
the bloom faded of red stains
on the fouled pavement
under the green door;
the clean machete with plastic ribbons round it
like roadworks,
the plain-clothesmen
hatching something in a leather jacket,
maggots for bait perhaps
or the unlikely reductive process
of their logic
under a brow of white knuckle.
Criminals or young people
had been passing the crack in plant tubs:
the police comically just missed every time.
The noise of the club,
through repetition, gathers mass,
it is smoke on the point
of becoming solid
with figures trapped inside
gesticulating for a future
where the power soars in the head
and spills out.
The sky an afterthought,
a parasol keeping its distance,
passing by on the other side.

But in the dawn, across the alley
from the stacked crates of empties,
hundreds of sparrows chattering
in a Russian vine draped over a factory

reminded me of a school canteen.
Let that be his memorial,
whoever he was.

Purpose and industry: Dalston 1991

Caught in the snarl-up,
from behind your demister
you watch the schoolboys dealing
in the doorways of the convenience store.
Life's rich tapestry, you think.

Behind a skip off Gillett Street
big boys on little stolen bikes
pick up their envelopes from a shaman
at the wheel of a big car.
There's a feeling of purpose and industry.

He slips into the skin he employs
to harness the illness of others
like a giant corporation does,
at ease when some things
fall out of focus.

In the grip and thunder of music
under narcotic overhangs
his strides are disproportionate
through the market's hills
of litter people pick among.

In the washrooms of the towers of the City
just a mile away,
worlds above the subsoil of the Blitz,
the pupils of some little dealers with a habit
flare and dilate.

They flit silently in soft soles

forty thousand feet above Libya,
watching the flames in desert wells:
just so, they watch over us
through the night.

We are unaware of their white noise.
The shifting of currency quickens,
flickering above the closed land
where lightless farms boil dry,
their supply lines reduced to an absurdity.

Here in Hackney, see the coherent
chain to the distribution of the crop
in the alley where they have boys
to look after the cars.
No need to understand

the needs of goats, now, anywhere.
No need to be stacking shelves
and losing face. There's not much
to be heard for the clacking
of credit cards in the bushes.

The heads are razored to the bone,
telling you the skin
is a brief tent draped over rifts.

Giving them what for

1

County Court

It's the incompetence
of repossession that sticks:
the sometimes conscious absurdity
worn on a sleeve,
the incredulity.
Estate managers tanned
and tied for the day –
they are ill-rehearsed
and their figures are wrong
but the responsibility
sits easy with them.
A barrister stoops
above the mill of peoples,
angrier than his client
to find himself here,
shouting questions at a Greek
to make him understand.
A woman with the Koran
has a look of fearful delicacy
aware of every flicker of nonsense,
every downward pull
of stale tobacco and sweat.
Sending cheques to her mother
in North Africa,
working for her doctorate
she doesn't belong here:
there's one every morning,

a moment of satisfying clemency.
A fallen advocate from Pakistan
has a vest beneath his shirt
that reads 'Yellow Pages'.
A woman with her son and her friend
are giggling along the pew
as she contemplates
the testy Registrar with mottled hands.
Eviction's like losing your blouse on a horse.
Her son says he'll clean cars on Saturdays.
An Irishman stamps from the Court
shouting 'Ah well, Oi'm off to Choina' –
an embarrassingly private statement
and it somehow fits that nobody's listening.

2

The Leaving Do

There was a murmur of envy
as you announced the abandonment
of your career, because
there no longer seemed any point
to managing homelessness,
to containment
of the need for containment.
A curtain swayed by the French window
that opened on the devious yard
of possibility, with its sky.
You left a roomful of appreciative drinkers,
and progress,
and routine,
and the sharper creases and the shoe-polish
under the table.

By the exercise of nous

and the firm look you conjured
from somebody's mother,
your job was to avoid
the need to sort the feckless
from the stricken:
but when the chips were down,
to cast them out.
You had to dress up to do it.
Those you had managed
expected little of you:
it was for this shame you were paid.
Now those who have the character
will be battle-hardened
and ready to rule and draw hard lines.

In Eastern Europe, people believed
that the homeless camped out
through choice in the West.
Who chose the verminous sleeping bag
and the whispering lung?

The friends you met
coming the other way,
     resigned to getting on,
      their dispatches memorised
    or making their plans in silence
    on the up escalator
  took this stumbling feint
into the U-bend of the future
before emergence,
holding their bunch of violets
up like an Olympic flame,
burning away the gases,
brushing the wet hair
and the lost words
out of their eyes.

Misrule, Towyn, 1990

With a clatter, the sea pushes
its tongue through the letterbox.
It does not empty or relieve itself.
The Axminster rises towards the ceiling,
passing a barometer half way up.

This is my home and I'm having it back
from the sea: swilling up to the front room sill
and window-frame, newly reglossed
in duck-egg blue, forty years of marriage.
Grateful to find there are knickers intact
on the top shelf: one pair fresh
as rising dough on the hearth
and I'm ready to meet my maker.

Hers is a small house
in a silent gallery of snow,
in a plastic capsule won from a cracker,
broken soon: a hermit crab
darts below the swirling fall of sand
among the surging levities of beach-plastic
and the shoes that feel life returning
in the bedroom.
The rattle of shingle
is uniform and triumphant
across the kitchen floors of Towyn.

On a roof anchored uncertainly with planks,
there were ovals of grey ice
on blue plastic sheeting
like lakes from a plane in blue mountains

as I lean down from an early meal.

My son asks
if it was like this in Atlantis,
a little water
riding together suddenly
over the flat of his hand
as he lowers it in the bath,
knocking the houses over, like this.

I must have been twelve or thereabouts
when I pored through the atlas,
speculating what would be left of the uplands
if the sea reached six hundred feet,
recording it all meticulously
as the sea blustered
not far from the door:
the West Siberian Plain,
the basin of the Ganges and the Brahmaputra,
the Fens, the North European Plain,
most of Cheshire –
was it the fury of clouds I wanted
or simply disorder,
was it a sad end,
was it a just desert
or the little death
that sets a story in motion?
The strong winds rage along the isobars
and people begin not to notice
how it plucks and tears at awnings,
raging at bars,
perhaps more that it did before.

On the way to work,
I noticed how the buildings
loitered in the street,

how I could have stopped
and watched anything happen:

it was a sharp cold day,
people ran to the river bank
as a shack approached
and floated slowly past:
at the open back a boy and a small girl,
between them a dog with its back to the water,
the boy taking pulls of a cigarette,
the girl holding the tip of the dog's tail
between her fingers in the same way,
pale and very concentrated.
We were left gawping.

We felt our ways
upstream and down
for something familiar.

But now you cannot retreat as far as the sea
you belong to
because it will come for you.

Ciudadela, 1991

Under the stretched skin of the houses,
under the whitewash
facing the sharp sun over the rocks,
under the sheet binding the jawbone
the dreams are obscured.
The televisions are off
like cagebirds with blankets over them.
Wakers turn to reach
familiar points
of reassurance and pleasure
where they are to be found.
Aimless hymns are gathered into the sky
from streets deep in shadow
where the smell of the baker
and the early bicycles remain.
The first components of the town's
prayer of noise under the sun
are cocks and mopeds and the secret
plume of a fart under the sheet.

At eleven the sun holds my head
in its grip,
a thing detached in its lap:
there is no comfort of reference
in the quickness of the lizard
or the sardine or even the bells.

Take me in, to the upturned boat
of stone on the horizon,
the fresh breeze, the thanks of green
in the glaciated valley,

the hand on me of that.

By one, the fish are a triumph,
running through the glades.
I watch them till the water
rises in my mask,
the little schools that graze
and synchronise, dart
and flock in the grainy diminished light.

The sun's a watery ripple
on the surface of the ceiling at four.
Street voices surround me like cold air.
The ceiling fan draws me up.
Blue-white legs have stirred the plaster
and are propelled out of vision;
their scrotum or light-bulb
is a towed anchor.

Dusk: a man disgorged safely
on the sand, if he can find the right sea.
The rhythm of the other sea in the shallows
does the moon's breathing.

A couple are up to their shoulders
in the bay: the other sea
explores their limbs
fast together
as tongues in secret explore each other.

The doors of the year, well done

Up Balls Pond Road the turkey's
speeding past the window
where the Eyyup Ercan Mustafa Brothers'
sausage in batter's left for dead.
Straining through the door-frame
full of ebullience,
it takes to the cognac like after-shave
in readiness for the solitary honours
of the oven.
                    Stuffed
with prunes and apricots
it'll agree to anything
like some half-remembered uncle.
Our cat Snowflake bites
digits at the edge of madness,
faced with the deadpan requiescat
of the sealed container
where the turkey slumbers
like Sir Walter Raleigh, his ultimate night
no less fruitful in its way.

Gorging is deeply ingrained
to force the window of the New Year
and to make the Sun come pink again
blushing a few minutes above the horizon
the colour of a hung turkey
to help us sleep easy now
towards the buds in the snow.

May the last supper
with its judicious shower of friends

last long, the turkey flushed and full of itself
and the Queen allowed in again
after all these years
to say that harmless parody.
May we forgive our parents
as we forgive ourselves
within the bottles
of our sloped shoulders.
May we grow politic, mellow
and forgive our little replicas
and the poorer years:
but first, this morning,
the expected spoiling of toys,
the glow of obtrusive joy,
the hopping from foot to foot
at the grey crack of dawn
as we insist on the revenge
of the watched kettle
before the grating tear of paper
and the crows of delight
by the black grate.
And awake on the gradient of morning
the root vegetables
coming smooth in my hand
amid your fury of industrious love.

Like a minute of impending snow
the turkey in the oven
darkens and whitens.

Unwritten chapters
for Peter Finch

In which	the audience doesn't warn him
In which	he is in heaven, and for eternity he doesn't love the people he thought he did
In which	every cloud has a blind horse
In which	he does not know that a cloud is rising behind him
In which	he jumps over the fire all night, and is sick in the end
In which	he is taken in to the architecture of the trout
In which	the poets write better history than the historians, but it is not the same
In which	he cannot do things he knows he can do
In which	the most familiar room cannot be entered
In which	most daylight has a velvet ear
In which	it's a short wolf that sees an ant

Tŷ Newydd

A supple, determined V of geese
follows the line of the surf,
knowing September into the stiff wind:
flecks of whitecaps above them
reach to the indistinct hinge of the sky.

I listened for that hinge:
my whisper came back to me
like the surf across the railway line
and up the hill, but it was busy, busy,
building hypotheses,
stakes for the heart.

The memory of power
brushed me, and I thought
of the day I first dressed myself
and I stood up
and surveyed the distance to the floor
that pushed up towards me.

Then the paradox of generosity
called by
in a daydream of a place
where people lock the door
and leave the key outside
in welcome to the unexpected guest –
or - with the stillness at my back
as I turn away from the empty room –
locking the inside in.
So I climbed away:
there was a delicious cold sweat

under my shirt for the wind to play on.

There were green shoots among burned
heather in dense cloud, and I heard wings:
they were the flutter of brown paper
unwrapped in another room:
they were the poetry shut in,
with misgivings, a concealed offer.

amlwch: n.abundance; also, a small town
on the north-east coast of Ynys Môn

The very idea of identity involves fantasy,
manipulation, invention, construction.

Edward Said

Note on pronunciation:
'ch' is pronounced as in 'loch' for Scots, or 'Bach' for musicians
'w' in Chwm is a short 'oo', very roughly as in 'look' in the South of
England, or as the Northern English pronounce 'rum'.

al-Chwm

1

The place I grew up is called abundance.
My not knowing Welsh
was not knowing this,
flowering in adulthood
one side of a fissure.
Circumstance and time
are two thieves shaking with laughter
but in other spheres I trudge
toward responsibility
for truths and lies in language,
sitting on the verge
at times with my bags.
This is written in the wind:
why not here?

2

Half a century of cataracts
over round stones that were eyes
to heaven, of water chuckling
minutely through stained brickwork
and I emerge into al-Chwm
with a sudden jolt of trust
with the relief you feel when you explode
out of a tunnel in the Underground
to a crash of leaves and speed and light,
the roar's end.   Then a quiet animal
homecoming.

3

al-Chwm is an inversion
of fulfilment and language,
mindful of children
growing up displaced
with their years not rightly focused,
and those for whom
the simple is at first too obvious,
who can only ride a bike
with a partner looping up and down
on the other pedal, on a steep hill
with a bend at the bottom,
and there's traffic.

It comes from an inability
to look abundance straight in the eye.

4

al-Chwm's a town on a concealed point
that comes to you when you're ready,
when the mist lifts, stripped of its poison,

a town that strains at the leash
that slips out of my hand.

Entering al-Chwm

It began and ended with the barking of tethered dogs,
a hundred street lights for the non-existent carouser,
nobody up who was up to any good
but nobody was up,
footfalls exaggeratedly soft in the house,
the fridge appearing to boil defiantly
in its limelight,
ordinary things reversed
in a town like any other
that had never slept, nor ever would.

A man carries the place he comes from
on his back as he unravels,
it is transformed with every step as he is.
Others in his peripheral vision
shift their shape, but it is always he
who is running through a defence
with a mazy run that slows
and the game ratchets up to a blur
of speed and wonder, the tackles come
in a series of thuds within him
and he is on his own,
the commentator faded to their mutual relief,
and the judgement:
he was meant to pass the ball but didn't.

He is reconstructed as he diminishes
by schoolmates he hardly remembers
who have carried him forty years without noticing,
by the milk of human interference,
and he carries their vowels for them

that jostle for his attention in gatherings.
Friends wrote a different essay
when they were eleven
and collide a second time
in the same time and place,
their electrons and neutrons
arranged for a different party.

He drifts, not noticing
the decisive moments under his feet.
The town he turns in to is al-Chwm
with his pancake stack of faces
that consolidate to the one book
with its pages of flour and disappointment,
dried milk and prevailing smile
collapsed into each other,
with his waiter's tree of dishes
for the approval of the town he's made
that will come out to meet him.
Many meals, many traces, but the dogs
bark for each other, not for him.

This is al-Chwm, they say:
it is permitted to drop unnecessary loads.
There are memories he will declare
nothing to declare, green channel
and there will be nothing we can do.
It appears that what happens is allowed.
He finds the people of al-Chwm
wear mirrors on their clothes,
their currency is uncertainty,
their traditions rich
but indistinct.

Their monuments leave much
to an imagination shaped

carelessly by weather and time,
preserved for a minute that lasts.
Their songs resonate in the memory
as in a dome – it's acoustic
rather than detail they celebrate
though there are fragments
strangers recognise,
and those they bring –
it's not clear which.

Those who seek refuge here are safe:
the code for acceptance is a capacity
to raise one eyebrow
and they have joined you, or you them.
Thus a concern for justice is unknown
which brings much relief,
and al-Chwm is immaterial to the Fall
which fell past it, unobserved.
The parallel has replaced the afterlife.

The al-Hambra rescued

In al-Chwm, the world's wonders
are given a break to recover
from all the prying and footprints and exhaust:
they lie disregarded in the fields.

The al-Hambra is abandoned and forgotten,
shifted stone autograph by autograph
to the site of a chemical works
on a promontory, where lichen and moss
were an aspiration in a boom of foghorns.

The subtle Arab gardens
move up and down again
on pulleys set beneath the waters
in forgotten ways, hanging
and fragrant, facing cold peaks.
They are still about heat, but its memory,
and the memory of an inquisitorial
staring-mad rigidity,
a suppressed unhappy childhood.
They are replenished
with subtle rain and desertion.

Overheard

There is no divine authority
among the people of al-Chwm;
but they have heard the song
and know they will never enter
the changing labyrinth
of the lark's throat.
Inviolate authority's invested
in a moment of that throat,
its gracenotes thrown loosely
but as they fall they are adamantine
then lighter than air again,
a riot of butterflies
moving across a valley.

The meaning of terminal

Is it a terminal condition?
Is it a retirement home?
Is it a utopia?
Why should I answer my own question?

No.

Its dynamic quality, cunning
is common as dirt here
in the cracks of its stones
and between toes,
it's built on watchful stillness
amid the intricate
dance of its insect life at dusk,
the learning of thousands of sudden
changes and close calls in flight
and then abandon, negotiating these,
it's all in the deep wrinkles of those
who stay a winter season.
Between high and low cunning
the al-Chwmian aims pretty good,
from practice
clever in circumventing.

For the young the days
are a circular growth,
a relay that lengthens like tree-rings
while the years shorten.
When you come round again
there's always someone
or something waiting for you

and you grow in the comfortable
oppression of villages, watered
with unnoticed ambiguity
until you need no faith.

Below the surface, a stillness
related to what's below tundra.
Therefore al-Chwm's fertility
is slow, and its seasons.

Some way off it is driven past
by a man from the walls
of company and sound
with a concealed memory
of miles around him.

Later, al-Chwm will be heard
in a cricket whirring feebly
two valleys away:
it can minimise itself like a screen.

Then it may rise to a shout
but he will not be there then:
al-Chwm will have passed him by.
His mother said no when he asked why.

The property of dreams

While I was dreaming in al-Chwm
I bought a house.
I tried to master
the reverse siesta,
waking briefly
to rehearse my dreams,
find my house,
put it in order.
Now we drive toward our destiny.
For a hundred miles of motorway
a spider clings to the wing-mirror.
A family wait in the house:
for them it has served its purpose.
You want to supplant the lives
out of them, and you realise
why purchase of room
is a capital offence in al-Chwm
which means your spirit dies.
Beware the fulfilment of dreams.
As you reach the doorstep,
in an act of heroic and loyal
self-harm, the space vacated
by the vendor may collapse.
Stand with your back to them
and your dreams will emerge
as neighbours, as stubborn
and brave spiders.

Hindsight

There's a room of transition
at the slightly shabby end
of a branch line
closed years ago,
where you are visited
by an embarrassment
of sins of the heart.

They are persistent,
those old adolescent
crimes of meanness,
the seeing another's individuality
or hunger as a shadow
that became a lead ingot
in your ageing pocket.

Still they bring you
the small presents
that diminish you,
they know no other way
but the way
of the mirror
of the act.

There's sometimes
no need of forgiveness,
as when you pay the bill
discreetly in a restaurant
and turn away,
that is, if ever
you have the wherewithal.

Just enough

The once unemployed hang about in the square,
so many, to be taken in lorries
to the Elysian fields where they will work
three hours, enough to feel good
as promised once in the white heat
of technology: the hands hard,
the blood coursing, a vigorous
Sunday joint on the table,
vegetables you have dug
and no weariness:
the promise of the millenium.
al-Chwm's up
for some kind of prize
but the judges get lost,
it's too small
like a best kept station
with no line but a platform garden
and there are so many silent tracks.

Through surfaces

You find yourself
dipping through surfaces to al-Chwm,
skimming
across a flat calm
under skies of stratus.

Your craft is a flat stone
small enough and round
to fit in the crook of a finger,
and you think hard with your eyes
shut, because everything about you
is contained, of St. Bridget
who made the crossing
on a piece of Irish turf
to al-Chwm, and continued
on her miraculous course.

Having gasped for breath
all your life under wave
upon plausible wave
of unnecessary explanation,
you are cured of the need
to know who the skimmer is.
You don't want to know who did it,
the butler in the scullery or the fairies,
with a bloodaxe, a rubber glove
or a serpent in a tree
or an ingenious combination
of all three:

there's no tall explanatory boat

to carry you away,
just a hard little body clutched
and spun, the sound
of the spray, the speed
and meticulous angle
of a hard surface
that doesn't quite penetrate,
over and over beyond
what you calculated possible
and you dip below,
sink with the finely
varied oscillation
of a feather,
discover
another kind
of play of weight and lightness
or miraculous discourse.

al-Chwm's lacunae

1

An attractive village,
a well-worn shoe:
its scuffs are memories
or nurtured cares.
Books are not burned
but brochures are
because they spill the beans
till there is nothing left

but a vulnerable secret.

2

The bigger the state
the duller the senses,
the smaller the pigpens,
the blander the mushrooms,
the more desperate the crocodile
conversing on the hill,
the lonelier the need
for the penetration of space.

3

Nevertheless in one history
al-Chwm expands
to the size of Siberia
because half the people of the world
want asylum there

from the other half:
in this way it shadows
America, pumped up
distractedly beyond sense.
As a warning to al-Chwm
the weapon of the world's aspiration
is turned on America,
to which it has no answer.

4

The two paradigms of power
that gave the individual
the blessing of an intimate regard
were Stalin's
and the great American penetrations.
al-Chwm follows a policy
of standing up against a wall
hoping that no-one will shoot
or ask it to dance,
then that a long decline
will prove attractive
for which the reward in al-Chwm
is to be left alone.
It encounters
the conundrum of Venice
that required full exploitation
for its decadence to flower.

At this point the account
breaks off,
reappearing pages later
to describe a village
of the same name.

As always,
the durable answer
is fragmentary and brief.

Kinship

al-Chwm searched for the Arab kinship
audible from the name
and could find none at all,
so little it seemed as fishy
as the disappearance
of the magnetic pole
over the next hill,
and the next.

Only later they discovered
DNA in common
with a small Saharan people:
great humidity out of the arid,
the underlying kinship of opposites,
like solidarity
only dancing in spirals.

They shared a meal of their different gutturals,
their tonalities
and their different teas
and afterwards they walked in a vaulting space.

Forgetting

Through the years the fame of al-Chwm
spread like slow gum
on a forest floor
and hardened,
causing injury to the fauna
that did not adapt.
Each dawn it was reinterpreted.
That way the place was not followed
and found freedom.

Things began not to work,
there was a rash of compensating
mechanism, which failed
as well.   Spiritual growth
occurred in inverse ratio
to convenience.   The demand
of competence stepped on heels
no more.

An undiscovered fold
in the cortex of the brain
came to prominence,
a faculty of stubborn parody
of half-remembered science
generating flightless
craft that made sense
like the dodo
only when thrown,
and enigmatic sandwich toasters
that could simply not have been true.

In time, capillaries
starved with long bewilderment
thinned and withdrew.
The fold was left open
to the wind in the brain.
It turned generous as wool
on a memory of barbed wire,
grew reverent before stories
and began again.

Moments

Houses in al-Chwm
have a book of oneness and moments.
It is all right to wait,
for the book to be
composed for a while
of blank pages.

Families read from it
after dinner, often
gazing in silence
at the empty page
like a sheet of cloud,
the young no less nostalgic
than the old
who are no less full
with a fierce longing.

These are not books
of the hurried notes
of industrious people.
There is a moment
when the wind is at rest
and nothing moves in the undergrowth,
and still nothing is committed to paper.
Nor should the wine be turned to vinegar
through long fear of the exposed line.

Moments that led to wrongness
are particularly valued
and catalogued.
Though furtive,

such moments allow their faces
to crease into a smile
when they are recognised.

To know when to choose them
is to transcend,
not time,
but one time,
one time at a time.

al-Chwm chosen

Their hearts sank.
There was this intersectional chink
of time and justice
in a perverse cosmos
(for a twisted universe is possible
without a personal god
with a history,
like a twist of lemon
to embitter it)
where they found
they were expected
to judge the others.

Britain was its own mis-shapen asteroid
spinning clumsily
with an atmosphere
as you would say
she entered the room
and there was an atmosphere,
and this patronised village
with its untracked record
was obliged to judge the others,
man, woman and child
(as the meek shall inherit,
and don't ask
what happened after).

It refused:
nothing happened,
there was the silence
of angels passing

till the cog slipped
on to another winner
whose subjects
might not be so fortunate.

Corkscrews

They learned to disassemble
their molecular structure
like a Loony Tunes cartoon:
screwing themselves up
into corkscrews
they would go,
kerpow!
through vegetable matter at first
then brick
then hard rock.
Their first experiments
were painful,
but through long years
to understanding the liquidity
the bones need
to swim about the body
as in an aquarium
of fluid outward form,
they added the physics
of karate and Merlin
with a fixed ambition
that served them in the end:
they would fling themselves
and land on the grass
in some unimagined continent,
panting with uncontrollable laughter,
dying like swans,
crushing a cowslip bell
where they lay,
exhibiting, I'm afraid,
little curiosity

and much cliché
but astonishing the inhabitants
with this difference
from the destroyers of the New World:
their vice, their tabaco dorado
was the point of singularity
where all the laws break down
and nothing outward is changed.
Like swallows
they always knew the way home
to al-Chwm.

Game

They learned
from the nervous Scandinavian deer
they herded
about fucking on the hoof
then being off again
almost without breaking stride,
uncoupled,
unhinged.
It evolved into a game
of rushing and patience
that combined
mental and physical power
and letting go,
and letting go
that made for a strenuous landscape,
its prospects
erotically charged.
The indoor version
was a great success, played
from room to room
of great public buildings
made for the purpose:
they used it to cleanse
their parliament at recess,
to restore the supple joints
of their politics.
For spectators
it shared the shortcoming
of motor sport:
as the protagonists flashed by
to another room

you had to imagine
from the sound.
In their decadence
both the game of sex
and the parliament
were competitive,
grew fractious
and burdened by too many rules.
Short cuts were devised
through the chambers of arousal
to the rutting room.
Some old timers complained
of a loss of discipline,
others remembered
joyous abandon,
and how absence makes the heart.

Long shot, last throw

This working model of a man
is made like a brick shithouse
all the better to fight
for good living space
and fertile land;
this other with a grasping reach
the better to get at the delicate
precarious berries
or to gouge the adversary.
Made this way partly to instil fear,
together they are more than their sum,
though not by so much.
If they are small they thrive
because they are nimble
or alert, or can see far
or can advise or command
with force of mind,
or are gifted in hiding
or their sperm have a particular drive.

Now, when the clay tablets
have electrodes attached
and evolution's not a rising plane
but a horizontal line
to a state of wave and cable,
self-referential
and eventually dipping,
an interesting fraction
of these qualities
are in demand.

Much of a species
gone beyond its point,
we adapt with a customary
brilliance:
the road to the coronary
is a kingsize burger away
for the humiliated primate
zapping its remote
in a memory of adaptation
from back when the low status baboon
just got on with it
and died of loss.

Men have nothing to lose
but their anger
and there it is,
spilled over the road,
petrol,
do what you will with it,
America.

al-Chwm tries to take a position,
cornered and truculent,
arms folded,
the choice seething with maggots
that will cure wounds
and will have you:
either go back to the animal,
the whole accident
of collaboration
with an ecology
millennia beyond reach now;
or, slack-jawed before the box,
there's the suckled victim
in the free, humiliating cardboard hat,
yearning back to the coloured planet

he believes he came from,
but not this one,
                        that one.
                                        Then,
behind the rows of pudding-faces,
always
the unacknowledged face-puller,
the furtive glimmer
of awareness
with its sporadic flare-up
that threatens others
with a knowing provocative look
it can't hide, try as it will.

That is what endures
biding its time
face to the furrow
as long as it can,
blocking out the cries,
its heart a rare
subversive jewel.

Nightmare

There was a dark period,
a perverse marriage
of mind and sense
when leaders were chosen by smell
for their intellectual power:
a brimstone odour
of concentration
that putrefied
and decomposed
to superstition.
That which is not the progress of sceptics
interspersed
with long moments
of balance
slips back toward nightmare.

Who is to tell the difference
between stagnation and balance?
There is always a stupefaction unit
in fine uniforms
who watch for the momentary wise,
to stun them like flies
and who wish them a horrible death,
drowned in their own lucidity.
These are the revenant souls
of a sniffer dog drug squad
known for their devotion to crime,
to their nightsticks
and to living with the shifts of certainty.

Beyond anxiety

1

Hidden in their preoccupation,
the work they did in a time
they did not yet inhabit,
the staff at the hospital
grew distant.
The day was made
of successive ramparts
that a very small memory
played behind.
Patients colluded,
their look became glassy
above a retreated core.

Someone rediscovered
the remedy of touching and grooming.
They needed too
the skill of solitude.
The nurse would lie down
with the patient
and it became unclear
where one ended
and the other began,
as the cat spread out asleep
on the place of anxiety.

2

An epidemic of decisiveness
and acceleration
corrected itself
with a spontaneous freezing of crowds:
visiting strangers
would wander through them a while
and suspect a theatrical happening
or the commemoration
of an armistice,
till they caught on
with a yawn of relief.

3

They turned up
a yellowing paper
from one of those golden dawns
on the use of social systems
to suppress anxiety,
defeated later
according to other fragments
for the clumsy optimism it was
by an empire
that overcame its victims
with a wall of irresistable images
and slavering want
that reduced them
to a fatally uncritical mass
and turned them against themselves:
resistance was killjoy
to the seduced
and was exposed to the full panoply
of the media-political complex.

A fable, surely
yet in al-Chwm
they strove to evade it
with vigilant exercises
in derision, followed
by a periodic raggle-taggle caravan
in pursuit of the constellation
of their hopes.

After weeks of hard travel
(and to die on the journey
signified arrival, threads
to pulsating stars)
they'd arrive at a rock face
where the arrangement of ropes
obeyed a change in gravity
and the climbers were pulled
toward each other
in an unexpected configuration.

Always,
if they travelled far enough
they would encounter strangeness
at a face of rock
and would take nothing away with them,
satisfied.

Entire hospitals
would up sticks
and do this.

Variations on the ear

1

Music

Their shudders laid down track on track
of counterrhythm, snare and airbrush
as the depth of their dependency
dawned on them:
they would die
if their personal music were taken away.

The backlash was
cold totalitarian turkey:

gangs roamed from house to house
destroying the speakers
that spilled music
from across the world
across the room,

and just in time
before it was reduced
to a syrup of uniformity,
a desert of earwax.

So they listened as the sea
roared and sighed
for months.

So, listeners morphed
into performers, thus

the audience
was liquidated
in time and in circles
that heaved in the form of waves:
the least musical learned
to tap out a unity
that was always in the air
on household instruments,
spoons, milkchurns
and catgut for which the cat
was venerated when alive.

From under the earth
with the sound
of a burrowing of moles
came strains
of ancestral music
that summoned the skill
and the work and the pleasure
that begins before you can walk,
lost voices and the plucking
of strings that meander
away from keys and back
into affirmation
you think is terminal,
that bubble up from the grave
with a distant sound
of subterranean picks,
of a liquid that pulsates
on through the body
till it reverberates
like a bell in the cranium.

To turn the soil of music,
enforced isolation
and a moment of savagery

were permitted, it seems.
Innocence grew again
like trees dressed
with candles and sequins
on still nights.

Hearing music on a breath of wind
they would die to be inside it,
driving it with their hips
and the sounding board of the palate
to affirm a greatness
in the small sound of the animal,
in the near-silence of ants digging,
the near-sound
of the blood in their own ears
and the deafening song of the fly
with whom they shared
a deviation of chromosomes

and therefore stories
exchanged over a piece of meat
half-burned on the fire
and left on the sand,
and they listened to the bass
throaty drone of limbs
that vibrate in darkness,
finally the fly's almost silent
dance of bodily unguents,
of the dawn of anticipation.

Then there was the pepper
running out from a clandestine radio
hidden under some flight of stairs
under the stars,
crackling into life.

2

Turbulence in music

al-Chwm had restless wells of talent
that emitted swarms of things
the population didn't want to think about:

so a background of chatter
and clanky music
soothed the internal voice,
moderated the performance,
shaved the concentration,
slapped a safety certificate
on the memory.

It's an industrious nation
that lives off sustainable argument,
the manufacture
of tranquiliser and enervator,
stimulator and distracter.
Under a brilliant onslaught
of the weaponry of the banal
conceived in a heartless library
soundless but for the humming lights,
the suppressed
stream of consciousness
became yet another bunk-level
in the cellar of the unconscious.

People would go crazy
without their implants of music:
left to its own devices
the irregular rhythm of nature
struck them as a moral terror
run amuck, with its disorder

and its punctuations
of elitist silence.

And yet, since both
fashion and natural selection
reach out through a sequence
of mistakes for the variable,
the adulterated, the perverse
(one a little faster than the other,
both in the form of a flattening spiral
where you expect to see
the misfortune of others
and which there were hairdos to celebrate)
there grew an irresistible fixation
for the artifice of silence
over the humdrum.

In a paroxysm
of self-induced panic,
in the altered state
of hunger denied,
for the good of the nation
in a precipitous revaluation
after a run on the mind,
sonic wallpaper was banned.

Governments collapsed
in an anxious, shallow-breathing parody
of the origin of species:
under the first cabinet of a new regime
they played funereal music
with subdued flourishes
on the radio, then as the radicals
gained confidence,
the only permitted broadcast
was a gnomic poetry

with little reference to anything
anyone knew,
an island of five minutes' speech
in twenty-four hours
of tuning to a hiss
you could turn up
and scour for variety.
The population fell
on the minuscule ration of words
and devoured them,
regurgitated and chewed them again
like shoe-leather
till they were satisfied.

The storyteller who seized on
the twisting, evanescent phrases like flies
with a predatory quickness
and recalled the words
with the tongue of a striking lizard
was king of the quiet wastes.

Shutters were opened on faculties.
There were motorways of silence
everywhere
that led them to memories
of the savannah
when they dropped out of the trees,
rightly made
to be vigilant and afraid,
picking up the stories in the grass,
distinguishing the sounds of danger
from the soft garrulity of the wind.

Circuits were in recovery.

There was a wall of mountains

behind the city
that had not been seen before
which some thought
was the placing of its humanity.

Deadly or not in al-Chwm

Anger was a rare incursion
but ire, that prophetic fury
was another matter
in the weather of the place,
upending tired thought
and blowing down boundaries.

Envy was brought by in-laws
from elsewhere, and withered
before a disinterested poise
located in the pelvis
and the nape of the neck,
that showed in the walk.
Some said that when the walk went,
the seed of envy
started to germinate again.
Old age strove to retain
the walk in the mind.

Sloth had its season
in youth and age
but was valued in the prime of life
and was a branch
of the study of time.

Lust, why not, peaked
like an erection
in a history lesson, distractingly,
then followed its declining curve
sometimes bucked
by joyful exception.

Gluttony was dependent on supply,
but formed part of the science
of intemperance
which suggested a remedy,
a ruptured circuit made good.

Pride found its own level
mocked beyond a certain span
or understood, through the mechanism
of a safety valve,
to be self-mockery
whether it was or not.

Avarice
was a simile
for unfulfilment,
its original meaning lost.

It was said that in early times
these things were subject
to a septennial audit
by an authority
which had slipped away
like the state at that time,
or the time in that state,
whichever.

Textbook history

1

Once they'd mislaid
the climate that made them
what they had been
centuries before,
they were few, and depended
on the known individuality
of the other.
Such was their cohesion
they forgot their place
and their identity
was in their wandering.

In time again they settled
and from a perceived
homogeneity
there grew an assertive flame
of purity, its origin
diverse as you like,
a new configuration
small,
concentrated
then churning outward
like a cloud of lies.

2

Your whole past flashes by

The oceans were thinking collectively.

Outnumbered cigars
played poker for the desert
and the flooded land.
Their cards had no faces
or aces.
Collateral damage was again
the lot of innocence.

Farmers woke afloat in a storm
in a mute laboratory,
victims, they believed,
of some malign intelligence
which turned out to be their own.

Seafoam flying
on a hurricane
reclaimed an old imagined freedom,
unbought, unsold,
to be savage –
to behave in a manner
unrestrained by the stays
of civil norm;
of culture unfamiliar
to the established powers;
to be ungoverned;
to be fair game,
to restrain trade
since you fail to imagine goods
when they have no narrative
you have contributed.

The watershed festival at al-Chwm

The nature of time
was the eye of their storm.
They celebrated the momentous day
of the discovery
that time was not linear
and had ceased to be thenceforth,
when they set aside
the discredited question

    answered by death, or

    answered by the flat wages
    of merely banished want
    with its storeyed carpark
    of arrival,
    the finality of its wad
    of never completed floors, or

    answered by the monotony
    of a final justice,
    sister to that of the chosen faith,
    each as corrupt as the other
    with their need for the damned,
    the gilt and kitsch of the leader
    and the led, the same bloody harp
    forever, the torturer's mantra.

Ah, progress,
shot down by the curvature
of the spine of time,
when what they realised they meant

was a starting point
decent enough to return to
after a day in the fields.

And every year the ceremony
of the slipping in and out
and then the breaking
of the keys to an imagined road
to an imagined capital,
the shedding of the absolute
with a queen of uncertainty
masked for one night
with a rubber face
who confirms them,
or does she,
as laughing and skilful
lovers of time.

The first symbol of the night
to be worn is the painted eye
at the back of the head,
so there can be no denial.

The second is the bicycle
denoting the curve
in the track of time,
how they follow it
like a rear wheel
as the road is made
and they are part
of its ingenuity.
Turned around
and placed on the nose
it's a pair of spectacles
and the spokes make the eyes
multifaceted.

They would carry elaborate
representations
of the vehicles of seeing
to a central point,
and the burning spokes
would turn them to trance.

Through the eyes of insects
in the heart of the night, renewal
does not need the stamp of humanity.
The revellers know
they are consumed in their turn
by the small, the numerous
and finely tuned;
and as the harbingers of day
creep indistinctly
with the dew of their cleaning machines
over the debris of broken masks,
a cup on its side, an empty bottle
and an abandoned wing,
it is they who know
with the first rays of the sun
that just to see it all with better definition
would be something.

Certainty

1

You cannot account
for the movement
of all the bacteria
in every shadow
forever:
there is always one
that will bide its time.

There was this critical loss
in the quality of attention,
when the pinch of irony
slipped through the fingers.
Once the smile stopped
playing on the lips
there remained
only an absolute
to pass on to the young,
just one flat stone
without which the sea
would be drained.
al-Chwm was gliding
into the dock
of the state of error,
in a downpour
fast and furious
of unintended consequence.
Thought to be decayed
from lack of use,
the organ of surveillance

took on its own life
and those of others.
None of the positives
of careless abandon
apply here.

2

al-Chwm was the place on earth
where lifeskills were supposed
to run deepest
where fools were thin on the ground
and the detection of bullshit
and self-interest
was at its most refined;
where cures lay
at your feet
like diamonds
to be chosen,
or infections
to be farmed.

3

al-Chwmians discovered
in the eyes of others
that the way they lived
was the object of desire.
At first they were uncertain
whether this was flattery
or distorted by mirrors,
but disproportionate power
made its bed with vanity
and lay in it with clouded vision:
there was a flight of steps,
whether leading up or down

no-one could tell.
This policy was embarked on:
they needed children
with dark-rimmed eyes
and ill-fitting trainers
to bring out the best in theirs
who showed signs of indifference
and etiolation, it was thought
through a decline
in the incidence
of clutching hands from below.

They imported little bony refugees
with a business sense beyond their years
who had seen their relatives gunned down.

This was the attraction
of the client state.
On the horizon they could see
the dust of its coming.

With the new children
came parents in traumatised postures,
the domestic and industrial
cleaners of the world,
bred to be peasant farmers
but as ever both more knowing
and more innocent
than those they cleaned up after,
sustained by a hope
that it was still the right valley
they were trudging across,
one they knew would grow deeper
between two mammary green hills,
tumuli that spoke before
of crops as much as death

and would again;
and through the investment
of a dying generation
they were sure
their children
would ascend the other side,
look down from beside a pool
and choose to remember
or forget.

4

Predictably, there were tensions
and a border hardened
like a scab that had grown powdery
and flaked away when left alone.
Blood from faces
that had pressed against the window
ran underneath it:
centuries ahead
walkers made a path
from the composition
of its soil.

The building of frontiers
stimulated the economy
with all the things that feed
prickly exteriors
and the fear of subversion
that sustains them:
there was opportunity
for border guards
and designers and cutters
of uniforms, manufacturers
of nightsticks, infra-red
cameras and sewing machines,

creating more demand
for the flexibility
of migrants, more
of the debilitating frisson of threat
and the ancient desire for police.

All around, with the force
of a theorem, as the fear
of resentment grew
so did resentment itself,
thought to be mitigated
in the client states
by the value of currency
from those who had left,
but reinforced in truth,
every banknote
given a twisted face.

5

How does the positive shift
come, the collective sigh
that says a decisive 'enough'
as ever more darkness
approaches, piling
on tense mouths
experts thought
regressively
less generously set?
To put forth green shoots
from within an outwardly
functioning regime
that demeans the majority
is an inexplicable gift.

There's a moment

of critical force
in the ground
that provokes an avalanche
or an earthquake
or the tyranny
caused by one educated person
too many
who opened his mouth
at the wrong time:
this one came
from the collision of tolerance
with deep-vein self-interest.
It was the final grain
that dropped on an accumulation
of weariness, the floater
in every process
that puts progress in reverse
or full ahead,
that discovers the energy in the rest.
It was triggered
by having it up to here
with being told that to be generous
was to be weak.

6

The hope now
was to rediscover
the al-Chwmians'
legendary gift for analysis,
for spotting smooth transitions,
sand in the machine
and remote light:
rather than strengthen the border
as the early migrants,
who would have slammed it shut

behind them, demanded,
the belief grew in removal
of the need in the client states
to uproot.

Descriptions began
to come in
from beyond the edge of the map
on tracks that led back to the heart
as to a peeling kitchen door,
beside them
the occasional abandoned culture,
the invisible counterpart
of rusted tanks in the fields
and the unvalued faces
that lay behind them.

From these traces
they began to acknowledge:

the loss that came with accumulation

the scorn in themselves
for themselves
they had sown in others

the slow things they had put to the margin

the redundant body parts
found later to be essential

the plants despised
and found to be medicinal

the memory in the fingers
that with forgotten skill

made a trembling bridge of yarn
to a people
not yet deciphered –
then the divine restraint
not to intrude

outside the ramparts
of their own achievement
that had made them passive and defensive,
the capacity
to listen with generosity

that there is no way back:
there is only attitude

they were in love again
but this was a second marriage
with uncertain contours,
small unrecovered settlements
and the unguarded expressions
that inhabit them:
they would spend a portion of each day
searching the lines in others' faces
watching for the clouded eyes
of foreigners to clear.

Bookend

Here are the ironed features
of the end, mounds planed
by the hooves and rain
of centuries;
the stones of al-Chwm
lifted bodily away
to build centres of power
with ever cleaner lines,
taking with them unbeknown
their stubborn blemishes.
There is this desolation
of reeds wheeled upon
by the wind,
bristling and swept
in a complexity
never repeated,
that stretches away
to where sky and distant hills
part company,
the earth's curve
creating an illusion
of open possibility.

There have been layers
of obliteration, the removal
of defining features
such as the nose of the place,
its capacity for insight
and delusion,
collective and individual.
There were people who knew

how to live here
and nowhere else.
It's what made them
vulnerable and envied:
caught in the headlights
of the invader
they would stare back
with an amused tolerance,
frozen forever
in the illusion of arrival
after a good meal
surrounded by friends.

They got their wish
to become elusive again.

This was an unfinished copy
of heaven, with half its qualities:
you will never be done
working out which half.
Things fade off uncompleted
like the tail lights of a thief
disturbed at his work.

From *Surfacing* (2012)

Dipping through surfaces

He had lived a stack of years
that he could see
though to his horror
half way up some blurred.
The stack became a tree
made out of disks,
its branches glimmering,
groping for the dark.
Some were appendices
that still bore data
for an abandoned settlement.
Some represented years half-lived
that glowered in the trunk;
all that remained of others
was a pulsing spark.

He wanted to be several places at once.
Not in them, but the places themselves.

There were tunnels that interconnected,
burrows with sand brushed down
from the roof by passing heads,
through the years each grain and gobbet
threatening greater collapse.

There were the usual cold inexplicable
channels of air, and tired air
that had settled in the branches
of numerous lungs,
passages of lifetimes not only his

159

that breathed under the turf.

Some he had built
but old strewn paths were more interesting
approached from the unexpected,
tunnels that converted to lofts,
a figment inhabited
beyond the talent of his clumsy hands.

Refuse delineated
some departed current.

He wanted brilliance from the subterranean
like a man with his own mine:
he did magic
and he wanted to be taken in by it
but he was truculent with his own
concealed pockets which having sewn
himself, he could predict.
He could not live by illusion
with love burrowing its way through the hill
momentous through a wall.

The machinery and then the museum
was the point of the mine
but then he knew
that to live outside the truth
is to hear a flooded ceiling bulge
but to live within the truth
fades it and creates another.

One more denial joined a distant line
that was approaching very slowly
ready to come in a rush,

all the opportunities
he had not known to take.
It was time he brought them flowers.

He looked through the denials
in the attic again,
at the the racks of mannequins
in fur coats rising through the house
followed by bears on a string
that had to be kept out.

He wanted something to have stirred,
perhaps a movement of the whole attic
suddenly cantilevered out over the sea,
the flaked paint blinking in the light.

The opposites in his life would not fly
together seamlessly, they fell away,
they were single wings.

Outside, relief
when visible waves came up to him
through the turf, like a wind under a field
there when he asked.

The Second Crossing

He turned on a thick grey
Dunlopillo mattress
after punishment,
and picked it in consolatory bits
that accumulated on the pitted concrete floor
of the outhouse, surrounded by trunks
with old toys in them, and bedsteads.

It was one of those unexplained
misdemeanours that had escalated,
something to do with wet clothes put on
and he was leathered for his own good,
the house on tenterhooks
for the arrival of a separated brother
which he upset.

For his encore, carried upstairs
by a thin-lipped aunt, he turned
and plunged a short arm
down into her cleavage,
into the dark line of mystery
and bafflement under high
and buoyant meadows –

though never so buoyant as it seemed
at the time. He felt an evil freedom
and the rages in the house were dominoes
as he lay there and he thought
still young among the heaving of his sobs,
cleavage, I'll remember that,
although the word came afterwards.

His brother came to make peace
late at night it seemed
and he feigned sleep
but then he woke and smiled
and they charmed each other
and were forgiven for nothing,
the adults circling far out like whales.

There is a moment
that defines aloneness
when you fall asleep in the outhouse
where the strength has to be found,
the source of refuge in a theory of justice
to be tested and found wanting,
not to be blurred with sensation

like the whistle of leather high through the air
or the sound of a motor across the sea,
but the motor seized and driven.
The wind tries to lift him in his car.
He is as heavy and protected
as a fish in a river,
he is nearly immobile in the current.

Outside, a quarrel of plovers,
the oystercatchers drilling for more land,
the orbit of bees hurrying before the wind.
The sudden appearance of lands,
hump-backed, as quickly
boiled away in the dazzle of a flat calm.
Memories no more than dimly understood.

He will neither take anything for it
nor sell it for consolation or cure.
Huge, unquiet, meant to last,
the amputation of childhood

is half-done, a half-bridge
beginning in the middle of the strait
with steel rods and sinews stirring out.

Spirits of the place

The strongarm women
whose flesh was beginning to hang in folds
smiled and wrinkled and filled
the canteen kitchen window:
they had grown wise in the cabbage-steam
above the open drains.

They were the only ones to relax
with the little boy who was not all there:
they leaned on their pyramidic elbows
and looked down as he added to the steam
with his pee and looked up to them
with his tiny dick between finger and thumb.

Surely a sign of madness: the headmaster
lost everything he thought he meant
when this little voice rose up
and called him a fucking cunt,
clear as a dropped coin
on bathroom tiles

and he fell on it, we heard and felt
something dangerous and adult
roll towards the edge beyond just
beating, and it went on
too long to count
until the infant teacher

reached out a defiant arm
and extricated him
through the gaping silence

round his introspective tears,
the cutlery suspended
in a hundred small hands.

Above his head the teachers pealed
then wrangled and he was released:
the women in overboiled
sky-blue pinafores waited for him
at the canteen window,
the closest things to a benevolent god,

their world-weary impatience
grown formidable in judgement
from the density of their pre-Christian hips,
non-conformist to the marrow
while authority lay in the hands
of a pale unresolved man,
stalking the tables.

There was a meal set out
before him, out of the silence
behind their chatter, their shouts
over the pans that trembled: for potatoes
there were rocks piled on a plate
at the end of the field,

a miracle of igneous green
when it rained, as if they were not ripe,
the drink a harbour
deep and empty, waiting for husbands
off the North Atlantic convoys.
Who was to say it was a poor meal?

Their wire wool and bleach put away
and the churns of pigswill ready at the door
they gathered and leaned out

as the monument of progress
lay for mending
at his feet before them

and the lessons drifted over the grass
from open windows.

Ethnographic Museum, Budapest

1

Their marriage dawns with the twentieth century
and you can almost hear the bride's underwear
creak like a glacier unburdening itself
as they look forth defiantly
over the blanketed head of a photographer.

The groom's right-angle stance
sets him at odds, not to be tangled with:
there is something callow
about the need for this;

to her he's a catch though,
there will be a proud collision of bodies,
can't wait, you know this from the way
they look out at us, looking in at us too

on the nonsense that time is,
the broken crockery of it.

2

Next to them another pair,
she with an innocent wide
prairie of forehead,
trusting untested eyes
though is that a speck of fear?
Hard to tell.
He doesn't know where to put himself,
inserted in his costume

for the photograph
which is proffered over the years
to every visitor.
Blinded a moment
as he comes out of the sun
from his peppers
which are what he loves,
he hesitates before the picture
then reaches for it.
Acclaimed by the escorting village
they were, it walks with them,
forever as far as they know.

Elegy for Betty Hutton

In your Mom's speakeasy,
just as tall on tiptoe
as the greasy table-legs,
you belted out the numbers
up at drunken men
whose faces loomed and flushed,
and glasses clinked, and cutlery: oh
what a pair of lungs at ten.

Your family hounded and broke
in Detroit, your wake-up call
insistent as a bell, you had to be
the little bigmouth now,
sassy with lipstick
as you put yourself about in bars
to feed your Momma's habit,
explicitly relied on, hardly aware
of the premium of trust.

Long, long life by fifteen:
the break came, early and at last
with the big band, Vincent Lopez
and His Orchestra.   Just a kid.
The His a capital, like Jesus.
He had time for you
who were hard work,
little star hoofing it always
and only to please us:
all of a sudden
Let's Dance, Fred Astaire,
Dorothy Lamour.   On the trapeze

in The Greatest Show on Earth
eyed stolidly by Charlton Heston,
he of the freedom of the gun.
Diminutive and difficult,
always a determined diamond,
always pressure.
                    Then fallen
incomprehensibly far.

Full of yourself, pushing your husband
on the studio: Paramount push back
harder, on and out the door.
That unscripted jink a bit unsteady.
Fairweather friends thin out,
old demons gather,
unreasonable demands.
Go home and sleep it off, Betty.
You step out onto air.

And wake up having lost it all.
 Washed up star
that drank like a fish:
 now housekeeper to a priest,
astonishingly not a role.

Banished the flounce.
Breakdown, the driving nails
of humility.
                    A reappearance,
sixty-year-old smiling
hostess in a sports centre
in Connecticut,
with some of the old bounce.
Then surprising graduate.
I wouldn't call it a circle:
it was your curve,

171

Betty's originality.

I would have wanted you to know
that I was marked at four
by Betty Hutton's Annie Get Your Gun
in Holyhead: dragging my mum back
to the Empire to see
if Annie and the Indians were there,
and the Lion,
though you were all long gone
but for the Lion
and the Naked Man with the Gong.
Was that you in there?
Strutting your innocent stuff
through the dark to me
in front of the cardboard scenery,
behind the make-up slapped on
in all of the dazzling hokum,
you were fallen for:
caught with your cowgirl's lariat,
two horses, eros and laughter,
pulled my stagecoach,
propelled my Hollywood and Holyhead
short-trousered, spiky-haired confusion,
my future mangled Ben-Hur chariot,
out into the grainy light.

What comes around

Just as you convince yourself
that what the weather does
is teach disappointment
there's a molten crack of light
that slices the midwinter horizon
below the last bulk of advancing rain.
It's what you believe.

Exercising

Exercising
flat on my back
on the floor,
one foot in the air,

head to the bay window,
in the clear blue sky above me
pass three herons, slow
and upside down over Harringay.

Rare honey
for Siôn Evans, beekeeper

Black fur, bulk
of the dwindling bee.
Chambers of sweet rock
glisten, trickle, giving
and crystalline, long
after the ruffle of wind
on the flight home.
Power melting on the tongue.

Recovery

Now the thumping music
in my life's receded,
how the dreams lord it in my sleep
at last: they roam in packs
through the half-lit forest
of some purpose,
where the deep silence
that is always new
alternates with their yelps.
They drive and strain and flex,
they are wild and very clear-sighted:
they do not need glasses to check
their change.   One by one
they peel off and appraise me
with a look that shades
to indifference: they turn
and trot away
to munch among the roots.

Crowding

1

Wild geese navigate their way
by the hardwired stars
above unrolling grids of light
the length of continents.
Memory is stubborn.

2

Small birds in an urban garden
learn to speak up over traffic –
what do they need to hear about
but each other, territory, sex?
Now extra volume hereabouts
ticks her box.

3

Excellent silence
between planes.

The repeated hammering
of fine membranes.

4

Foxes and cats in the gardens,
the birds decimated.
Let the misanthropy rip:
we're a brief, decisive interference.

A balanced forest
would have little humanity:
those few
would be given a handicap,
a weight to drag
or a bell like a humiliated cat.
Ideal: a balance
of predators,
of killing, no fallacy
to see the momentary
beauty in that,
but no-one there to register –
why would you? –
how the uneaten move on.

Skylight

The skylight's just that:

lens to the fixed stars
over the ruminative clouds
the moon drives
in their indifferent grandeur
as if to milking;

little frame for the worlds
above my naked stillness
anchored on the rough cord
of a dark landing.

Hannah Evans discards a consoling cigarette

Barclodiad y Gawres: burial mound, 2000 BC,
near Aberffraw: 'the Apronful of the Giantess'

The key of the oiled gate
to the interior, to the spirals
in the dark, lies by the till
at the Spar shop where the keeper
has me sign and leave
a small deposit:
it's his act of routine trust.
Access to the tomb
was never so cursory
in the remote past,
but it's how we function:
as if I were looking
for a rented room.

The Spar shop's full of the glowing
sandblown skins of kayakers
in the fluorescence
of bright plastic waterproofs,
their eyes aglint with sealight
as they move among the shelves
of ready meals, these faces
that emerge from four-by-fours
with an organic, salty radiance.

Framed by lace curtains
in an upstairs window
gleams the polyester flag
of Liverpool: this afternoon

they're head to head with Chelsea,
some ungovernable
Saxon island in the Thames
now colonised by Russians –
they're two estuary sides
that flaunt their hoards of bling.
For some that's more immediate
than the immensity outside,
and for the better resolution
of the figures' hoofing
on the lurid turf, the curtain's drawn
on the sinking glitter of the tide.

The mound's gate faces north along the shore,
not out to sea, nor hunched away from it.
At some point in four thousand years
the reason's been mislaid.
Along the sightline is the flightpath
of the training fighters
from the base that fired
the imagination of my military solitude
of half a century ago:
I hold those Meteors, Vampires
and the Javelin and Vulcan
close in that recess where my play
delighted on destruction's lip,
somewhere deep in what I am.

The tales we bring have gathered
at the tomb's gate, where some wisps
of smoke drift downwind
from a patch of turf
that smoulders by the sea.
There were evanescent tears
before the thoughtless cigarette
that led to this. Underground

it burns for days, sustained
by rumoured gales.
Don't stir it up.
Better to leave it be.

Tales like hot stones dropped
from an apron at the gate
of the passage to the spirals
in the gloom of Barclodiad y Gawres.

Was it the dead who shouted
or the bereft lamenting?

The faces from the tales hid
between fingers of seafret,
voices muffled in the apron of the giantess,
whisked inland on spindrift
that diminished with them.
After the redress was inadequate.
And did a small abandoned queen
look out here with her streaming tears
softened by rain, forgotten by the wind?

When I am laid in earth,
may my wrongs create
no trouble in thy breast.
Remember me, but ah! Forget my fate.

The Shelveian Event
for Robert Minhinnick

That multicoloured swirl
was the coast of Shropshire
on the edge of the geology
of Wales when it was submarine.
For days I walked the shore
of the micro-continent of Avalonia
that boiled alternately
and ground its neighbours
till the Golden Apples came about:
Afallon, the Hesperides
beyond the gates of Hercules.
I watched the sunset's nightly change
of minerals, the green of all the limes,
the pink of all the shales of the sky
where Avalonia collided in the Shelveian event
with Baltica, and reared and bucked
five thousand miles in fifty million years,
still rising from the South Atlantic
in its slow, dancing, dreaming gale:
across a human lifetime it shifts upward
further on six feet northeast.

Thus Shelve's quiet hamlet
bears the name of greatness
thrust upon it
like an intercontinental Waterloo
where nothing might have happened
until something did:
                    the vaulting
at the great blunt blade of Avalonia's bow-wave
rode hemispheres on the slow

whip of the earth – that crushing, tearing,
gnashing, rupture and release,
the indiscriminate rushed packing
to expose curved backs of land,
among them the terrane of Shelve
shifted over from Llandrindod
to lie against and name the Shelveian faulting –

shovelled as we are, postman,
farmer, our future
spiralled in the trilobite,
the graptolite, its tuning fork
that rolled and slipped through the mixing
of the planet for our ears to ring
 one day and ache with the wind,
our eyes to map just north
of Grit Hill, Old Grit and the hill
of Mucklewick, Disgwylfa Hill,
its half-remembered language
postcarded through the scheme of things
from the sitting room at Squilver Farm.
And to the south of Corndon Hill
whose Ordovician dolerite
piped the hot verticals
that to this day mushroom its cowl,
the Hyssington Volcanic Member,
acid vitroclastic tuffs,
sandstones, wackes;
and dreaming in the south
of distant time, breaking rhythm –
the Clun Forest Disturbance,
the heavy footstep of its thunderous glance.

A January wind
carves across Hyssington Marsh.
The clouds are whipped away,

the sky is clear.
I stare for hours at the thought
of raindrops' impact, baked
for posterity in seconds,
fossilised with care on mudflats
one by one in the tenderness
of moments hardly yet materialised.
The storm passed on,
the earth is harsh,
and came to something here.

Performing Micah

And they covet fields, and take them by violence;
and houses, and take them away;
so they oppress a man and his house,
even a man and his heritage.
Therefore thus saith the Lord; behold,
against this family do I devise an evil,
from which ye shall not remove your necks;
neither shall ye go haughtily: for this time is evil.

Micah II v.2-3

Seven, not quite up
to the lip of the pulpit,
with the clear enunciation
that my mother taught me,
I pipe out the lesson
from the Book of Micah.
I'm invisible though mounted
on two hassocks,
unaware of the way
I disorientate:
the congregation think
I'm disembodied
but I'm not.
Under my cassock
I have schoolboy's knees
where the hair since grew
and wore away. My mother
proud at the organ.
If the truth be told
I'm smug, project well.

But there must have been a newsreel:
there's no other way I could retain
the memory of strengthening
brown legs in kibbutzim
or that renewing sun.

Decades on I uncover
wave on wave of dispossession
next to my small parading
of that text.
I milked the drama, I know,
still have a weakness for it:
like a sweet sucked
against the molar
I extracted everything
it might contain
which I think would have been
rhetoric, innocent of milk spilt,
torched rooves
and the door that swings
on a dusty wind.
So now I want nothing to do
with whoever said these things.

Congratulated
at the Sunday dinner-table
for (I think) precocity,
pride took to the veins
like Bisto gravy, grounding me
for a lifetime; the evil time
balanced with relief
amid a well-fed repartee.
Marking the page of the family Bible
I find the tip of a dried fern,
the spores long desiccated.
The faint pencil line

against the verse is true.
I think of the doorframes scorched
that Palestinians no longer
reach their children through.

Rockpool

The pool is barren
where my net tracked shoals
of shrimps that drifted,
darted, distracted.
Fifty years ago
it was a screen
I penetrated
and that answered back,
though framed with moss
and braids of bladderwrack
like an antique certificate,
while yards away, the tight-lipped
waves relaxed and died:
replenish, diminish,
was the sound they made,
a pulsing background static
ready to augment
as soon as I was ready
to a human voice
that would begin to spread
among the rocks,
when I was six.

If I had a hammer

She's West African, she's tall
and she rocks back and forth,
there are creatures crashing in her
to rein in, be they stallion,
devil, mare, devil-may-care
childhood trauma, England
trauma, husband trauma
and with all her strength she calls them
shrill devil, and they make the print
of her Bible swarm with riches
that are African and hers
before her song can soar
away from their clutches.
They had their own trees
to praise her by back there,
she'll never lose her looks.
She intones in a shady spot
in the park in her many voices,
it's taking weeks and she's beyond
fragility, today she's thousands of trees
by desiccated lakes.
Today it's a hymn,
half in the shrubbery
with her back to me:
My Shield and Defender
the Ancient of Days,
I remember the double-forte verses
rung out with the little childhood hammer
of my leading treble: the echo is complex,
there's freedom in there somewhere,
and other matter.

In the hoarse, lived-
and died-in voice
of a fractured
Christian soldier,
the bow-wave of conviction
cloven in the air, she sings it
in Fanta, Ga or Twi,
that's as near as I can get
without approaching her.
We've both left our shores
in our different ways, she
so much further, it seems
there's more she needs
to believe.   Hymns, too,
travel the air sometimes
meeting nobody, and grieve.

Feedback from the Assessment Centre

I'm too old for this.
Sweating but competent
I pass the numerical
and verbal reasoning test,
though I'm too aware of my feet.
Do they realise who I am?
But I'm old enough to know
that as soon as the generic *they*
turn up to be dressed down
I'm lost.
In the interview,
my wizened judgement
of the paths
combines surprisingly
with a stubborn late belief
that things – my things –
might work,
and so make something fresh,
with the clear eyes
of a man of experience
in driving spray.

It's by the roleplay
I'm rocked back,
in the lifelong incapacity
to think on my feet
when under attack:
this young thespian hireling
chief executive for the day
snacks me for breakfast
to demonstrate my lack of sidestep.

It's a primitive transaction
from way back where through red mist
I would retaliate without a strategy,
a neural disconnection
channelled into burning cheeks.
I didn't get the job.
I got feedback and sympathy.

I think of my father-in-law
under fire on the Normandy beaches
at twenty-two
laying out tracks for the tanks
above a toppled hulk in a hole
that had men in.

The morning after, the wind
still whistles in my pockets.
Returning to the old zoo
there's a few more cages empty,
the possibilities thinned,
more things I didn't do.
My life still stretches out before me.

Words

Don't get me wrong,
some of my best friends
are words,
especially my own.
There are more of them about

than there used to be:
they stick to your face
and drop to the ground
with odd numbers of legs
protesting at the air.

They don't string together
on the page and stay there:
like birds on the wire
they abandon you, autumn
can come any time.

There's no knowing whither
they'll be bound: perhaps
to the forgotten crossroads
where an adult's words
manhandled you aside

as you tried
to describe the thunder.
There's no ceiling to belief
in their power: what they say
goes before they wither.

There is so much hurt in words,

there are not enough
eyes in the world
to flinch from it,
those eyes lit up

that are looking hungrily
for words to do justice to them.
The words are greater in number
than the maggot or the starling,
than the sum of meaning.

Friends tell me, sit and listen
to what's there where none
penetrate, but they do,
through cracks and keyholes
and channelled down the wind

in the grass where I lie.
It's a wise man
who can turn away from them.
Even as I look up
the clouds are heavy with little ones.

Flock roosting

All my sense
of the fluidity of form
comes from the November
shapeshifting
of fifteen hundred starlings
for the mathematical,
valedictory joy of it:
they turn in on themselves
in a glove
that fills the whole
dusk above the water,
and out, and in again
but where is the hand they enclose
before they contract
suddenly to roost
on a passive black geometry
of spars,
reflecting on the day
in their small individual
darknesses
beneath a pier,
joined by diminishing afterthoughts
from afar
to perfect their form
which is hidden,
trembles, chatters and is still?

Dark energy

I was drained,
my juices leeched away,
the battery neglected.
I think of the Humber Hawk
abandoned on a verge
up on the Mynd,
of its return to nature
under the settlements
of dark moss on the rust,
and the buzzard
with its still wings
waiting for the furtive rabbits'
loss of concentration.
Even in the image
of abandonment, optimism.
Shadows in the fields,
earth clutching shallow roots
sympathetically,
unregarded bolts of darkness
hold things together.

Reaching for plums

In summer rain inside a plum tree
we two stretch and climb and reach
to loosen all the ripe fruits that we can.
In your hooded anorak, the moment's
concentrated in the oval of your face –
if mine's the same, our mouths and eyes
are seeking out, our faces smoothed
and soaked and shining as the plums –
our anoraks so out of fashion
they're no longer waterproof.
The rain drums at the plastic on our heads.
Our first kiss damp, but then the burning spreads.
The fashions wash against you and recede.
You came round again like one of those, and stayed.

Backstroke

The Buddha's eyes are squinting
at the sun across the field.
He seems contented in his alcove
and he smiles down as you strike
away from him across his pool.
The camera's caught the spray
illuminated, falling back, each drop
your consequence, as with your wake
attached, you pull away.
All motion, you create a symmetry
against the stillness resting in the wall.
At the end your white arm stretches to,
I look out from the shadow of a tree.
Your blonde hair's dark beneath the childish blue,
your parting cleaves a liquid paradox
of line and surface; as your movement
shimmers, flickers, thrashes, undulates,
your eyes fixed on the sky and what's ahead,
your fingertip just skims the apex
of my living geometry of deep content.

Gastronomy

The grape kiss,
its fleshy tang and sweet uplift;
the marmelade kiss,
the humble kiss of buttered toast
on the tongue
that prematurely
led upstairs again;
the white wine kiss
and its inexplicable
acceleration to cognac;
but the kiss I remember most
with its golden, resonant succulence
is the roast parsnip kiss.

The same place

The storm binges on after hours
through darkened isobars.
A tornado in Kensal Rise,
which rises as it must.
The wind is chest-thumpingly high
round the house on the hilltop
where you live, bathed in leaves
in their changing ways.
My love for the gale's deep-rooted
but this bracing howl's a test.
The timbers strain, the house slips
anchor, spins, slowly at first,
then I hear you chuckle under the quilt,
and I'm certain we belong within the same
point on the map, in the same
rumpled bed, on the same swirl of contours.

Anniversary

Together
we found a small apple tree
in the wrong place,
on the last ridge of dune
that faced mountains
over a sheltered sea.

It was in blossom,
surrounded by sand
that shifted through marram.
The apple tree said,
I will remain unexpected
for a lifetime.

Virtually

We were searching for clinical guidelines
from remote workstations:
you scrolling down for depression,
I for the cost-effectiveness of physical activity,
in the same website together, unaware
and separated by a river and a city
and a concentration.
But there's no dividing membrane
in the virtual world or the insistent kind
that will keep us apart,
and now you mention it I swear
I could see the outline of your hand,
your face, and then the imprints of our bodies
pressed upon the web.
They did at least maintain some opacity.
And were gone, carried away as you swam
with your easy stroke
and your personal mouse
through the airwaves.
There's a residual crackling,
something momentary, unrealised,
that would power a small town.

A Pair for Bodies

1

Our skins are so different together
under the bower of the quilt,
the suffused light on them
bringing them out:
what you call the yellow of yours,
what I call golden, with a foolish
eagerness that can't belie my years;
and mine, that hairy Celtic
butcher's white (to be particular,
an off-white that's informed by pink):
purity, surprise and gratitude,
these I find in the mix
of my skin's colour
only next to yours
under the tent.
What's more, sometimes
you scorch my bristles,
make me think.

2

The temple of the body:
both ours flaking,
some structural damage.
You don't get that presence,
the colour of the sun on warm,
warm stone in the late afternoon
without inspiration from the lives
that passed by it,

leaned on it.
Worth visiting.
But then we find
that due to the pressures of the attraction,
the wearing and tearing,
it's closed for a month,
for restoration.

Echo

You were the one I called.
You comforted me
as I paced a kitchen
more relationships ago
than I rightly remember.
I think I howled
with grief and incomprehension,
though it was my doing.
Not long after it was your turn.
I remember the swell of abandon,
not a hint of a future landscape
of homecoming, not a hint
of a promise that remained
unseen till it was too late,
like a view of the garden
from your window
while my attention was diverted.
Later, much more
than my fingers were burned.
It wasn't a question of a script
I hadn't learned.
It was a love defeated
and confused and young.

I still might not forgive
those self-important lyrics
that hung around too long;
but my immaturity
was the one I lived:
it was mine then
as you were not.

Thirty-six years
echo with incredulity
that I recovered you,
that we are ready
as we were not.

Heart

Why do I always remember
my mother's words
from her one encounter with you
that if I fell down the toilet
I'd come up with a bunch of violets?
I was getting over
the last cohabitation,
off and on the vexing bicycle
of love: it was the falling off
that wasn't any easier
but here was something different
she thought she saw
that made her throat catch for me –
this I knew she meant,
barbed and wise
and hopeful for a moment,
if I fell in love with you.
You were a smart bunch of violets.
I wasn't yet connected up.
Smitten as I was, I bothered you
as you drove, just out of your teens,
tall and still coltish as you sat
on your dignity at the wheel
of your grey little A35,
I not knowing how to put
my overflowing want.
Not driving yet myself,
I never stood a chance
and then a common strand
through all the rich young detail
of the women who came after you,

all that I didn't cotton on to,
was the wanting to catch up
with something vanished up ahead
that others had – a hurtful
dislocation, heartless in effect,
I realise as I celebrate
a perceptible beat,
an irregular, soft,
insistent uplift.

Missing double maths with you

We lay on a beach
an imaginary forty years ago.
It was not warm in your dream.
I was naked, you were in pyjamas.
It was a Monday afternoon
and you were missing double maths.
I was in several dramas.
You covered me with my dressing gown.
Just out of reach.

A compelling case

I'm moving in with you

so the white wine
won't sit past its best in the fridge
and will be taken under the lime trees,

so the bread will be fresher,
the grass always green
on this side of the hill.

I'm moving in with you

so you can tease the hairs of my skin
like a soft-fingered breeze

I'm moving in with you

because you need no double negative
to make a positive

because I love your multitasking
as you kiss me on your way
to the recycling box
with a milkbottle, a jamjar
and a clean tin can in your arms

I'm moving in with you

because you're Miss Parallel Universe

because you welcome me

in my entirety

I'm moving in with you

so we'll make love
when the day of the week
has a d in it,

because you laughed so much in bed
that your ears were flooded with tears

I'm moving in with you

because a pair of jays came to your window
with their sapphire flash
and disreputable air,
and the nuthatch and the green
and greater spotted woodpeckers,
and the foxes looked up

I'm moving in with you

so our offices will come
within hailing distance
but we'll keep our discipline

and because I can tell
from your carbonated glance
fresh as the experienced dawn
as we pass maturely on the stairs
that we'll have a bit of a bundance

I'm moving in with you

because of our proximate exuberance

so I can write another poem
on my knees
at your ironing board

because the blood
has cantered, raced and roared
and is coming round again
for another tender tussle

I'm moving in with you

so the days will turn over
on their back,
look at the ceiling,
and whistle.

Padding back from a wintry bathroom

As I pad back in the half-light
from the wintry bathroom
I can see you've splayed out
in long, hidden spurs
beneath the quilt
across a frozen sea
of sheets to headlands
where I find your feet.
And when I point out
that you're taking up the bed,
you tell me drowsily that when I go,
you take up all the time and things –
skittering on the space-time continuum.

In the way you've opened out
contented over crumpled fields of sea-ice
there's this vulnerable generosity
I could reach down to take
and join with mine, the quality
of ease within me
that you introduced me to.
Informed with a simple gratitude
for desire, for your slow-breathing
angularity, my thoughts begin
to gather to a point already warmed.
Relieved of the nocturnal ache
of being fifty-eight,
the time's disarmed.

Discoveries

They pollarded the limes.
It was just before I moved in with you.
There was a wall of them
their backs to the hillside
and they locked our richness in,
blotting out the world
except for winter
and all we'd brought with us.
In the heat they made
living curtains for the bed,
and watched us.

Now their raw stumps are bowed
and arranged in attitudes
of possibility and victimhood,
bleeding the last
of the late summer's sap.
The barber-surgeons are in repose
in their afterfug of tea and fags
and Sun. The limes remind me
of the barber's shop on Saturdays,
the rapid fire of the scissors
and the windfalls on the sheet
now turned to an unremitting white.
We all, the trees included,
all resisted the temptation
to get up and run –
or did I, once I could?

Me moving in.
I'm holding off the thought

that unconnected acts
have meaning for us
with this sweeping back of curtains
to reveal the crops and bellies
of the distant fields
offered to wind and sun and rain,
the edge of London
spilling into Kent.
I give up, lie back
frowning at the thought
of disappeared complexity –
the squirrels puzzled
since they lost the limbs they ran on
or was it – could it be? –
the puzzles that were squirreled,
some of them to be unearthed
their living bodies raised
in exposed amazement?
It's the complicated
force of resurrection:
so many woods, who,
who would have believed it
so many leaves grizzled
and gone the way of the world
to be reborn, enjoyed,
the joy put back in them,
unlocked. The room
with a view of it's enough
for one who struggled
not to make connection,
wires in each hand
that yearned and strained
to lock into a living current,
all for the not-so-childish fear
of a spark and conflagration.

The room with a view's a hide too
with an eye for where the rim
of a flat earth pours
into imagined thickets
under a sky that stirs and deals
a vitality that's random.
I remember when I needed
to permit myself a wilderness
and couldn't find the word
but then I stumbled
on the meaning of encouragement:
you gave me heart and heard.
In that liberated space
I climb against the dusk,
and at my back the iron bar
of a black ridge gains mass
silently: I hurry on the gradient
but can't catch up
with the November leavings,
all the sun's last gifts of turquoise,
lemon, their fleeting scrawls
all out of reach.

Head over heels, hand in glove,
abandoning belief
in the magic single bound
to freedom I relied on,
just for once at one with the hills
and human, I'm observed
by a collective noun:
an intelligence of love.

The spotted leaves of some marsh orchids

I surface in the afternoon
from somewhere far away
and intimate, walled in
by lime trees offering green
hearts that flicker at the glass
in thousands. I am dulled
still from the place
we've met each other in,
that mood for being served
that comes with the confidence of both.
And next to me, you're off
remembering again
with your flowerbook, alert
enough to hold in sight
the shapes and hues of leaves
and blossoms from our week.
A difference in you
surfaces a moment, clear
as a roller from far out
I celebrate
as it washes over me:
your grasp of the particular,
what you see and I pass over,
needing to be shown
what's at my feet on my own land,
interrupted in the sweep
of clouds on my horizon.
I will glimpse a plant's complexity
if that – then it's gone again,
a fleeting stillness in the brush
while you are someone

with an eye that gathers,
who pursues, retains, resolves
and is resolved by this: and nurtures,
for all healing comes
from this precise desire.
I turn back to the leaves,
moved by the thought
that I might be seeing
the particularity itself
in another for the first time,
and I try to remember
nothing much:
the sea campion
asking for butterflies
on the cliffs.

In Sickness

1

As we drive west
through the winter solstice,
the lights blink at us
with their swift cold amber.

You are drawn and shrunk
with tiredness.   It's cellular,
your enemy, your illness,
it outnumbers you.

You need to understand
its grain and rhythm,
to observe, outwit,
and channel it.

We hurtle on towards
the valleys that have grown
to cup so much of us;
with stealth, we'll stalk

your shy absconded health;
together we will ease you up
from the cloudy riverbed
that calls you back, and walk.

2

Chamber Music

You set the resonance
of cherished wood
to mend the cell walls
that have blown down

in your puzzling interior storm.
It can't be done
with music that requires
energy it won't give back.

Which is a metaphor for us.
You find the room
for a generosity of mind
that overflows through what I see,

since like a drowning man
I found it in me
to insist on the surprising
value I put on my life

through you,
who'll be my wife.

River

Whatever the jostling,
confused intentions
that I harboured once
to have my way with you,
you feared the plaited river-ropes
of intimacy I proposed, and anyway,
I was unformed as water;
and the beauties in us
that we see now
needed to be shaped
with both our lifetimes.
We divided and the sandy bank
between us as we ran
became an island,
thickened, took our lives aground,
and grew trees, thickets, hearths
and London villages –
though with a city's substance
in, I insist, a division made of sand.
Provisional we ran; against all evidence
I knew I had the unifying river in me.
Currents that carried the seed
of memory of the other
past the continuing strand
as we wound on toward the unknown
shadowed water of the afternoon,
now we are together
and the weathered ropes of us
are twined, and roll and glisten
with a robust hope

that we still play thus
whenever the sea
may come for us.

Gathering

You're all smiles, you're
loving uptake, gold-dust,
precious bones.   But most
of all you're a bowl
of strawberries, blueberries,

raspberries with their soft silent rasp,
and rich cold yoghurt:
you have that appetising integrity,
the presence, the clarity,
and how slowly savoured.

It was in the way
you arranged the flowers
I brought you, your hands
and your attention
and your pleasure at one.

Our past begins to gather up
in sprays, to shape into
an unguarded wood;
it's full of birdsong,
wealth more than enough.

The way they swirl
about the leaves,
it takes only two
to create a flurrying
cloud of goldfinches.

Thursday, after making love

Footsteps and the rustle of clothes,
it's Thursday and her hair is drying
from drowned rat's tails
to electrified scarecrow woman
to presentable for the world.
The day's meandering
and you sink deeper under the quilt
and realise you have a smile
that's a mile deep
and it'll go about the day with you.
This is what would have been
if you'd dared imagine,
and it is.

The mistake

These days above my brows
that beetle, there's a desert waste,
all skin and bone.
It's where the mistake arose:

a scaly crater,
crenellated pillbox
waiting for a long-spent war
that beached elsewhere,
a simple life-form
here to usher in the end of time,
my lizard crest.

Primitive relic, lovetest
crowing that it's cancerous,
redundant till it finds itself a home
and a lease of life
not unlike me, its host,
or mistletoe –
but boasting a distinguished name,
the Squamous Carcinoma:
the epitome of scaliness
that squats on my head
like a puffed-up toad
babbling of hats.
May be a mistake,
but it's no misnomer.

Here death gets to ride out in the park,
rides well, could just spawn deluded cults
but passes on like an asteroid

with a silent whoosh.

An alien unicorn.

A nipple on a hill.

It's easily removed
although, no fear,
it's giving me a masterclass
of living in the moment: the taker
laying down the law to the maker.

Child of climate change
and hairloss, so there's no wriggling
out of my responsibility for this.

Go on, whatever you call yourself,
humiliate the last residue
of youth that hung in there
like an old man to a moving train.

But I'm glad to be living here with you.

The Harrowing of the Squamous Cell Carcinoma

He's quiet as a handyman.
The surgeon's inner mind
is muttering in dialogue with steel.
It's just his implements.
From the blue-toilet-tissue-covered
workbench that will drink my fluids
like the good earth, I can visualise
his concentrated frown – and near to me
(where's me?) I hear the process
of engagement of his stout blades
through the thick worsted fabric of my flesh.
Who would have thought the old man
to have had so much meat on the bone
of the cranium?

Later I laughed, like a surgeon
freed from the terrain of hurt,
with my friends in a soft yellow light
over rare breed Ludlow chop,
purple-headed broccoli
and the flesh of the onion,
transparent, crisp
at the edge, well done,
and eight staples in a tiny henge
to hold the dressing on my crown
with the precarious effect
of balancing a fried egg on my head:
such hoots of laughter as to strain
the gleaming tent-pegs in my scalp
until the dressing crinkled and became a flower.
Who would have thought, so many muscles

in his scalp responding to the old man's moods
to make him a magician?
So much laughter, so much pain and dinner
and my dear friends offering to stroll down
for me to the stationer's, for a staple remover.

Another day, down to the Injuries Unit
for the plucking of the steel-edged flower,
the unveiling of the plug: if only the nurse
could have shortened her tight-lipped
pause at the sight of it.
The images mass on the border of my identity
to redefine with the invader's language,
oh, and to enrich: the first wave left
fittingly to my loyal love, in hard words
there's a hole in my head
that a golfball would fit comfortably in,
echoing the surgeon's sporting imprecision
that he took a divot, one I presume
he grubbed out with his niblick.

I'm developing my repertoire,
my banquet of unnatural events,
my gabbling cure:
                    hit by a meteorite,
disqualified from the seniors' egg-and-spoon
for sporting an illegal declivity;
a water-feature, a mental birdbath,
here's a man to be cast out in an open boat with
since the dew will have a small depression
to gather in; a facility
in the top of my head for the third eye –
something to keep an eye on the weather, sir? –
and out of the top of my head
comes one of those whooshing,
ectoplasmic beams of light

and all the kids shout
'Ghostbusters' when I walk into the room:
the moment that I wish could go on
to the crack of doom.

I'm running the gauntlet
of the nervous glance
in the crowded train.
Then the dialogue in the dark
with a malignant absence, a heady rumour
ready to make do and mend.
And to reach out for another glass of reserva,
the reserves of humour.
It's so neat and round.

I choose to fall back on my supernatural relief
and its potent special effects.
Through the top of my head
I observe the movement of the clouds,
a kind of integrated lighthouse-keeper
here on my daily constitutional
in the hanging gardens of Horniman.
There are consolations, powers
as you wait in the gathering silence
for the first drop that will bring the storm
as when you know the applause
will come for the singer.
Here the City's towers group
and gather their reports of gloom,
their backs to St. Paul's dome; they appear
to be deciding what to do with it.
Above them rolls the storm, slowly
in its melting anger of dark chocolate.
Against it, far off, there's a string
of sixty white birds
pointed to Scandinavia, pearls

that roll and rearrange themselves
on the steep damp fabric
of the breathing clouds.
In that distance I detect
the earth's curve beckoning,
and uplift, downdraught, reaper,
reckoning, the beautiful
receding opportunity:
the animate high silver things
that strike without resistance
for the north,
whatever may lie there
or be the truth
or the way through the literal light.

Life with you

Life with you's
an intimately strange,
familiar thing:
enjoyed in turn
by future selves and past,

durable and welcome
as the buoyancy
of turf in a wild place,
weathered,
replicated, subtly
transforming, will last.

Being strong

Having to be strong another year,
another hour, we must be ready
for the sudden glare of the opening door
of all the griefs. They break in
and there's no answering the wind
that will take our soul or strengthen it.
We have a limit, set
in the unbearable barchart of the soul.

We're tired of the endless
muscle-shift when the ground heaves,
the planet coming up to meet us
and withdrawing its favour,
the steadfastness and bend
of the way of the trees.
We listen for the many ends
of the tree in us, the note sustained

to a point in the wood, the gust
that will bend us nearly past resilience,
will have us creak and scream
but retrieve a shaken equilibrium,
breathing fast, bound with love.
What's new is you remake me
when I break. Along the line
of the mend I sense

the light feathering of trust.

Spring

Viewed from above in early spring
the oaks have a shifting, softened quality
that gathers itself for green.
Spaced at our feet
the birdcalls rise at intervals
and the urgent, airy thump
of wingbeats punctuates
complaint with escape.

A rustle of wind
moves up the hill towards us,
recedes through the mix
of trees behind us, all
the senses awakened.

I had thought my capacity
for happiness was limited.
It is good to have arrived here
even if a little late,
discovering a language
I was exiled from,
waking with the ground
strewn with clouds and flowers
and images with their names
that are breaking cover, unafraid.

Notes and acknowledgements

These poems have appeared in *Anglesey Material* (Rex Collings, 1980), *Civilised Airs* (Poetry Wales Press, 1984), *Uncontrollable Fields* (Seren Books, 1990), *Selected Poems* (Seren Books, 1993), *An Elusive State: Entering al-Chwm* (Cinnamon Press, 2008), *Surfacing* (Cinnamon Press, 2011), *Late Love Poems* (Cinnamon Press, 2016).

A number of the poems have undergone minor tweaks, and minor or major cuts. A few have received substantial restoration, entailing radical re-entry to the original spirit. Two have been republished in renewed form: 'Industry and Purpose, Dalston 1991', originally published in *Selected Poems* as 'Shamanism, Dalston', appeared in Planet in 2018; and 'Community, 1982', originally published in *Civilised Airs* as 'From Waterloo Bridge, ensuing dark', appeared in its revised form in *Poems for Grenfell Tower* (Onslaught Press, 2018) under the title of 'Partitions, 1982'.

The last four lines of 'Hannah Evans discards a consoling cigarette' (p.178) are taken from Nahum Tate's libretto for Purcell's Dido and Aeneas (Dido's Lament) (1689).

Many magazine publications, too many to list here, are acknowledged in my seven collections. But I would like to mention my particular gratitude to three magazines that published and supported my work over years and at crucial points in my life: Poetry Wales, Planet, and Stand. Reaching far back, I would also like to acknowledge Fraser Steel, BBC Radio Producer, who in the late seventies received a battered cassette in the post of readings from Anglesey Material, and acted on it.

Lightning Source UK Ltd.
Milton Keynes UK
UKHW011431260319
339924UK00001B/12/P